Simply Sauces

Linda Gassenheimer

W. FOULSHAM & CO. LTD.

LONDON · NEW YORK · TORONTO · CAPE TOWN · SYDNEY

For Harold, James, John and Charles

W. Foulsham & Company Limited
Yeovil Road Slough Berkshire SL1 4JH

ISBN 0–572–01283–7

Jacket photograph illustrates
Poussin à l'estragon (page 50).

We would like to thank Harrods, and Way In at
Harrods, Knightsbridge, London for their help in loaning
props for the photographs

Photoset and printed in Great Britain by Input
Typesetting Ltd, London
St Edmunsbury Press, Bury St Edmunds, Suffolk

CONTENTS

INTRODUCTION

Sauce: '*Liquid seasoning to complement food*'

This description is the most succinct and probably the easiest way to explain what a sauce is or does. Sauces are the essential element that turn ordinary fare into elegant creations. With just the addition of a light, colourful sauce, a meal becomes memorable. The *saucier* or sauce chef is well aware that he is the magician of the kitchen. His alchemy is usually jealously guarded, as his creations form the cornerstone of any French dinner.

Sauces have played an important role in cooking throughout the ages. Marinated meat and cooking with sauces are mentioned in the Bible. The Romans used very salty sauces that acted as a preservative as well as a condiment. In the Middle Ages, sauces were necessary as food was very often stale or even beginning to rot. The history of great French cuisine is tied to the development and subtlety of its sauces.

Natural fresh flavour of food should not be hidden. In modern cuisine, sauce techniques have been modified to reflect this idea and to bring out all the nuances and flavours of the ingredients. Sauces have become thinner. Heavy use of thickeners tends to mask not enhance flavours. Sauces are used sparingly. Food should not be served swimming in the sauce. A modern sauce is smooth, light, glossy and delicately seasoned. The result is that you can taste the sauce and the main ingredient, as well as the play of flavours and textures between them.

The idea that sauce cookery is difficult, complicated and best left to professional chefs will, I hope, be dispelled by this book. In fact, the opposite is true. Sauces can be simple, easy and very often made in advance. Simple and easy is not only possible for a master chef, but for you at home.

Many sauces are made from a limited number of basic preparations. These sauce bases can be made up and frozen for subsequent use. With these well-prepared building blocks and other good quality ingredients, a superb sauce can literally be prepared in minutes. Especially when entertaining, anything that can be prepared in advance is a great help. Each recipe in this book gives pointers on how much can be done in advance, how to store, and how to rewarm your sauce. I have written this book for everyone who enjoys cooking and wants to create a sauce that is delicious, easy and elegant.

At first glance, French recipes for sauces seem endless – white or brown, hot or cold, there are hundreds of types. However, if one looks closely, a pattern begins to form. Sauces fall into groupings generally classified as white, brown, cold, and dessert sauces. Many sauces evolve from these groupings by the addition or change of an ingredient. As you use this book, I hope it will disprove the view that there are an infinite variety of sauces that no one could ever master. On the other hand, you can use them to provide infinite variation in your cooking.

Try the smooth delicacy of a *beurre blanc* together with a fresh light fish, or a hollandaise to provide a delicate touch for salmon or vegetables. Turn to a fine *Sauce Robert* for an accompaniment to a grilled steak or beef joint. Finish your repast with a delectable bitter chocolate sauce. I find when I serve this it evokes the comment, 'That's not chocolate, it's paradise.'

While these are probably considered the

'*crème de la crème*', they are but the tip of the iceberg. I often think mayonnaise and vinaigrette are no longer considered basic fine French sauces, because there are so many store-bought varieties. I urge you to make your own with the recipes I have given and taste the difference. Then explore the wide range of variations using some of the quality spiced or fruit-flavoured vinegars, mustards and oils available today. The aromatic flavour and interesting texture of a green-herbed vinaigrette, the freshness of a tomato mayonnaise and the delightful combination of tastes of mussels vinaigrette are but a few examples you will find.

White sauces are delicate, taking on the subtle flavour of an interesting ingredient. The creations are varied. For example, I use the unique properties of sorrel to create a fish sauce with a lovely, lemony ambrosia. Other taste sensations are produced by extracting the anise flavour from Pernod to accompany shrimp, or the apple flavour from Calvados to capture the essence of Normandy. Madeira, sherry, vermouth and whisky incorporated into sauces for chicken create sophisticated background flavours. For variety, there are recipes based on peaches, apricots, pineapple or cranberries. I find they add contrasting sweetness and colour to dishes.

Accompaniments to meat require more body. Brown sauce with its rich texture provides a key. I have included recipes which derive additional flavour from shallots, paprika, and the combination of mushrooms and port.

The fun of dessert recipes must lie in those wonderful ingredients: chocolate, flavoured custards, fruit such as raspberries, pineapple, apricots, or cherries in *Sauce Montmorency*.

Master the range of sauces available and you will delight your family, friends and yourself. My aim has been to create a style that ensures that I have time to savour these creations as much as my family and guests. Join me in enjoying the recipes of CuisinEase, my cooking school in Kensington, London. I hope you, too, will find it elegant cuisine with ease.

Bon appetit!

NOTES ON THE RECIPES

The recipes have been set out in an easy-to-follow pattern with special hints set apart. These hints have been included to help you understand why certain techniques and methods work. The aim is for you to be able to transfer this knowledge to other recipes using similar methods.

Measurements have been given in Metric, Imperial and American equivalents. You should follow one set of measurements only. They have, though, been based on the use of English ingredients. Thus, if you use these recipes in other countries, allowances should be made for differences in ingredients in these areas. Spoon measures are level.

Measurements for salt and pepper seasoning are a very individual taste. Unless an unusual amount is called for, the recipes say to add salt and pepper to taste. I use very little salt and recommend that you do the same. Allow yourself to experience natural flavours and fresh herbs as used in the recipes. Start out with a pinch of seasoning and then add more only if necessary.

Learning to sweat onions or any member of the onion family before adding other ingredients is important. This process takes away any bitter flavour the onions might have and brings out their natural sweetness. Also, it helps prevent curdling when a milk or cream base is to be added. This method is quite simple, enables you to do something else while the onions are cooking, and makes a world of difference in the results. See the glossary for the method and use it whenever a recipe calls for sautéing or cooking onions.

In most cases, just the particular sauce recipe has been given, but where the making of the sauce is an integral part of preparing the whole dish, then the recipe for the complete dish has been included.

GLOSSARY AND SPECIAL TECHNIQUES

Caramel

Caramel literally means burnt sugar. General rules:

1 The sugar must be completely dissolved in water before the water is brought to a boil. If the water boils before it is clear, the granules of sugar will burn and lump and ruin your caramel.

2 Try not to stir the caramel. Gently shake the pan. If the sugar washes up the side of the pan, brush it down with a brush dipped in cold water.

3 Caramel can be made by simply placing sugar in a pan and melting it. This can be tricky and I recommend following the recipes as given.

Crème fraîche

This is the natural fresh cream one finds in France. It is a heavy cream that is matured with natural ferments. It adds a wonderful flavour and texture to sauces and is not to be confused with fresh sweet cream. It is now available in most speciality food stores. However, a substitute is easy to make and gives excellent results.

To make **crème fraîche** Use equal amounts of soured cream and double cream. Mix these two creams together and leave covered at room temperature for 8–12 hours. It will become thick. Place in the refrigerator. It is at its best about 36 hours after it is made. It will keep for about 8 days in the refrigerator depending on the freshness of the cream used.

Deglazing

This is a method of diluting the concentrated residue left in a pan where meat, fish, game or poultry has been cooked with liquid – either stock, wine or cream.

Demi-glace

See 'By way of explanation' on page 15.

Sauce espagnol

See 'By way of explanation' on page 15.

Melting chocolate

Chocolate can be very temperamental. Here are some general rules.

1 It must be kept dry. Do not let any steam or liquid mix in while melting. Alternatively, if a recipe calls for melting the chocolate with a liquid, then use the exact amount called for. The liquid must be at least one tablespoon.

2 The easiest way to melt chocolate is to place it in a covered pan over boiling water. Immediately turn off the heat under the water and let it sit until melted.

3 Chocolate melts beautifully in a microwave oven. Follow the instructions for your particular oven.

4 If the chocolate seizes up when melting, a small amount of vegetable oil can be added.

Methods of thickening

Beurre manié Butter and flour are worked together to form a paste. This is added at the end of making a sauce to thicken it.

Egg yolks Egg yolks added to a liquid and carefully stirred over a low heat will thicken the liquid. If there is no flour in the liquid, special care must be taken or the mixture will curdle.

À la fécule Potato flour, arrowroot or cornflour are mixed with water and added to a sauce after it is cooked to form a thickening. The French like to use potato flour or arrowroot because this produces a glossy, clear finish. One rounded teaspoon/5 g to 30 ml/2 tbsp of cold water will thicken 425 ml/¾ pt/2 cups of liquid. Mix well, add to the boiling liquid and stir until thick.

Reduction

A liquid is boiled or simmered for a length of time so that moisture is driven off. The result is a glossy, thickened sauce with a concentrated flavour.

Roux

This is a mixture of a fatty element, usually butter or margarine, and flour. There are three basic kinds of roux: white, blond and brown.

1 White roux results from gently cooking the flour and fat together so that it remains white before a liquid is added.
2 Blond roux means to cook the flour and fat until it is a straw colour before liquid is added.
3 Brown roux means the flour is cooked to a russet brown before addition of liquid.

Sweating onions

Cooking onions until they are transparent is a useful technique. Sliced or chopped onions are placed in a pan with some melted butter or a combination of fat and oil and gently sautéed for about a minute. Then add some water to the onions and place a piece of greaseproof paper on top to cover. Place a tight-fitting lid over the top and lower the heat. Let the onions steam in this way until they are transparent, about 5–10 minutes. Take off the lid and let all the moisture evaporate. This allows the bitter juices to cook off and leave's the onions sweet and golden in colour.

Velouté

See 'By way of explanation' on page 48.

Fonds de Cuisine
STOCKS

Stocks form the base of most major sauces. With a clear, flavourful jellied stock a wonderful sauce can be made within minutes. If you have a freezer, then it is quite easy to have what I call a stock day. Make up a large quantity of stock and freeze it in ice cube trays. When they are frozen, remove from the trays and store the little cubes of stock in plastic bags in the freezer. Whenever stock is needed, simply take as many cubes as required.

Hint *They now have special plastic bags for making ice cubes. When water is poured in, it runs into little pockets in the bag. The bags then go in the freezer and when frozen, you can cut off as many cubes as are needed. I find this a wonder for freezing stock.*

There are several different types of stocks. I have chosen three basic stocks. From these any of the sauces you are likely to use for domestic gourmet cooking can be made.

General rules and hints for making stocks

1 Stock should only simmer, never boil. This means it should not go over 90°C/190°F. If it does, a muddy stock will result. You do not need a thermometer to measure the temperature. The water should slightly bubble on the surface, but not boil rapidly.

2 The water should wash over the bones as they cook. Thus, boiling water should be added if necessary to keep the bones covered.

3 Vegetables should be used in equal amounts. Do not add any strong-flavoured vegetables such as turnips or parsnips. One flavour should not be dominant.

4 Vegetables should form about one third of the total ingredients.

5 Use only fresh herbs. Dried herbs will give a muddied stock.

6 Do not overseason the stock. When it reduces, the seasoning will become concentrated. I prefer not to highly season my stocks. This way I can use them for many different sauces, adding the seasoning appropriate to the sauce.

7 Stock should be brought to the boil every other day if kept in the refrigerator. Bacteria grow very quickly in a stock. It is best to freeze stock if keeping it for more than a few days.

8 Do not completely cover the stock unless it is cooled. It will turn sour.

9 The cooking of a stock can be interrupted at any time and then started again later. I prefer to turn it off if I leave the house for an hour or so. Or I store it in a cold place overnight and continue the cooking in the morning. Each time I start cooking it, though, I bring it to the boil first and then turn down to simmer.

10 The result should be a semi-clear jelly.

FOND BLANC DE VOLAILLE
White Chicken Stock

This stock is easily made with chicken bones, wings or legs – either a fresh or cooked carcass.
The ingredients are meant as a guide. They need not be followed exactly.

Cooking time: 6–8 hours
To make about 3 l/5½ pts/14 cups

INGREDIENTS	METRIC	IMPERIAL	AMERICAN
Chicken bones	1.4–1.8 kg	3–4 lb	3–4 lb

Hint *Giblets, necks, feet and even the head can be used for the stock. The feet give an excellent gelatine consistency. Place in boiling water and remove their scaly skin first.*

Large onions, cut in pieces	2	2	2
Carrots, unpeeled and washed, cut in chunks	3–4	3–4	3–4
Leek, halved and washed	1	1	1
Stick of celery, washed and cut in pieces	1	1	1
A few mushroom trimmings or stems			

Hint *Do not use too many mushrooms. They will darken the colour and the stock will start to taste like mushroom soup.*

Bay leaves	2	2	2
Several parsley stalks, bruised			
A few sprigs of thyme			
Peppercorns	6–8	6–8	6–8

Place the bones in a large saucepan and cover with water. Bring to the boil and simmer. A scum will form on the top. Skim this off several times. When the stock is clear from scum, add the rest of the ingredients. Bring the stock back to the simmer and cook uncovered for 6–8 hours, or overnight if you have a reliable temperature control. Alternatively, it can be placed in a very low oven 100°C/200°F/gas low.

Strain the stock, cool, and place in the refrigerator. The fat will rise to the top and form a layer. Skim off this fat. Freeze. If it is not frozen, refrigerate and remember to take out and bring to the boil for a few minutes every other day. Bacteria form very quickly in this medium.

FOND BRUN
Brown Stock

Brown stock is the liquid obtained by boiling bones that have been first browned. This gives the stock its colour and nutty flavour. The cooking time of the stock depends on the size and quantity of bones used. With small bones, 3 hours is sufficient. However, with larger beef and veal bones it may take 8 hours. Thus, it is best to make a large quantity of stock and freeze it. Ask your butcher for some beef and veal bones. The beef bones give flavour and the veal give texture. Make sure they are cut into manageable pieces.
These ingredients are meant as a guide. They need not be followed exactly. In a professional kitchen, any leftover bits of vegetables are added to the stock pot which is always on the heat.

Cooking time: about 8 hours
To make about 3.4 l/6 pt/3 quarts of stock

INGREDIENTS	METRIC	IMPERIAL	AMERICAN
Beef and veal bones, half beef, half veal, cut into small pieces	2.3–4.5 kg	5–10 lb	5–10 lb
Carrots, washed and unpeeled, cut into 2.5 cm/1 inch chunks	450 g	1 lb	1 lb
Unpeeled onions, cut into 2.5 cm/1 inch chunks	700 g	1½ lb	1½ lb
Large leek, halved and washed	1	1	1
Sticks of celery, cut into pieces	3	3	3
A few mushroom peelings or stalks			
Bay leaves	2	2	2
A few sprigs of thyme			
A few parsley stalks, bruised			
Peppercorns	6–8	6–8	6–8

Set the oven at 200°C/400°F/gas mark 6. Put the bones in a roasting tin and place in the oven to brown for about 1½ hours, turning the bones half-way through. Pour off the fat a few times during this browning. Add the carrots and onions and continue cooking for about another half an hour.

Transfer the bones and vegetables to a large pot. Pour off the fat in the roasting tin and add a little water to the tin. Place on the hob and bring to a boil and scrape the brown solidified juices off the bottom. Add this liquid to the stock pot and fill the pot with water, enough to cover the bones. Bring the pot to the boil and then lower the heat and simmer for 1 hour. During this time skim off any scum that might have formed. Then add the remaining ingredients. Bring to the boil again and simmer for

about 5 hours. This can be done overnight if you have a reliable simmer button on your cooker, or it can be put on a low heat in your oven (about 100°C/200°F/gas low).

Strain the stock, return to a clean pot and reduce until about 2.5 l/4½ pt/11¼ cups remain. Let the stock cool overnight in the refrigerator and then remove the solidified fat from the top. Freeze. If it is not frozen, refrigerate and remember to boil for a few minutes every other day.

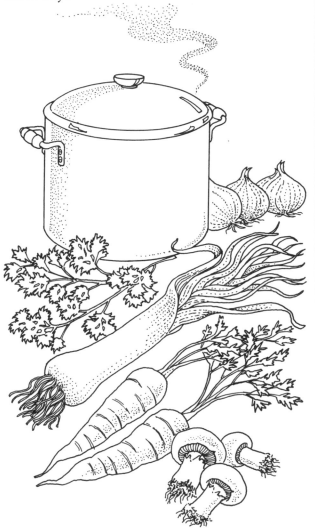

FUMET DE POISSON
Fish Stock

Fish stock, unlike a white or brown stock, is cooked for only 20 minutes with the fish bones. If cooked for longer a bitter flavour will result. These ingredients are meant as a guide. They need not be followed exactly.

Cooking time: 20 minutes
To make about 2.8 l/5 pts/12½ cups

INGREDIENTS	METRIC	IMPERIAL	AMERICAN
Fish bones, heads, trimmings (sole, halibut, plaice or any non-oily fish)	900 g–1.4 kg	2–3 lb	2–3 lb
Onion, sliced	1	1	1
Carrots, washed and sliced	2	2	2
Large bunch of parsley stalks			

Hint *Do not use parsley leaves as they will darken the stock.*

Bay leaf	1	1	1
A few sprigs of thyme			
Peppercorns	6	6	6
White wine	225 ml	8 fl oz	1 cup
Water to cover			

Rinse the bones and place them in a pot with the other ingredients. Bring to the boil and lower the heat to simmer. Simmer for 20 minutes. Strain. If a stronger stock is required, reduce the liquid after the bones have been removed. Cool. Store in the refrigerator or freeze. Bring to the boil every couple of days if stored in the refrigerator to prevent spoiling.

By way of explanation

There are two basic white sauces: a béchamel and velouté. Where béchamel is based on a milk foundation, a velouté is based on a veal, chicken, vegetable or fish stock often flavoured with wine.

SAUCE BECHAMEL
White Sauce

This sauce supposedly derives its name from the Marquis de Béchamel, the private secretary to Louis XIV. A white sauce was probably used before that date, but it was this famous food connoisseur who gave it its name. Béchamel is a mother sauce or *sauce mère* based on a white roux. It is a mixture of flour and butter that is cooked together and forms the thickening for the sauce. It is essential that the flour is cooked for several minutes to eliminate a pasty or floury taste. The flour is cooked slowly so that it loses its raw flavour, but still remains white.

The use of a white sauce is basic to many aspects of French and other cuisines. It is used as a sauce for eggs, fish, poultry, veal and vegetables. It is also a base for soufflés and cream soups. Because of its universal use, every chef seems to have his own recipe. I find that the recipe below is my favourite because it is easy and simple and always turns out perfectly. The sauce can be made in advance and kept for a day in the refrigerator, or it can be frozen. However, it is really best made fresh; and since it is so simple to make, I prefer to make it when I need it.

Cooking time: 10–15 minutes
To make about 275 ml/½ pt/1¼ cups

INGREDIENTS	METRIC	IMPERIAL	AMERICAN
Butter or margarine	20 g	¾ oz	1½ tbsp
Plain flour	20 g	¾ oz	3 tbsp
Milk (infused with 2 parsley stalks, 2 or 3 peppercorns, 1 bay leaf, 1 sliced onion, 1 blade mace)	275 ml	½ pt	1¼ cups

Melt the butter in a saucepan. Remove from the heat and add the flour and stir. This should give you a slack or loose roux. If the roux is pastey or tight, add a little more butter. Place back on the heat and stir for about 1 minute without colouring the flour. Meanwhile warm the milk with the infusion to tepid or blood heat. (This means when you touch it, it feels neither too hot or too cold.) Strain the milk into the roux all at once and stir over the heat until bubbles appear. This will cook the flour further. The sauce will be thick and shiny. Add salt and pepper to taste.

Hint *If you are not going to use the sauce immediately then place a piece of plastic wrap or buttered greaseproof paper over the top of the sauce to prevent a skin forming. Or, gently pour some melted butter over the top to seal the sauce. When you are ready to use the sauce either remove the cover or warm the sauce and stir in the butter.*

The sauce may thicken on standing. If it becomes too thick, then add a little more tepid milk to reach the desired consistency.

By way of explanation

The description in the brown sauce recipe on the next page is a significant reduction of the 600 years of evolution of French sauces. In deference to France's greatest *chef-sauciers*, Taillevent, La Varenne, Menon, Careme and Escoffier, a few more words seem appropriate.

Brown sauce, demi-glace, *Sauce Espagnole* Brown sauce is based on a brown stock which provides flavour and thickening. In a sophisticated brown sauce, brown stock is reduced by half (called a demi-glace) and is thickened with a brown roux where the flour is very carefully cooked to a russet brown colour. The original demi-glace used ham for additional flavour. Menon gave the name *Sauce Espagnole* to demi-glace made from Spanish ham, the best available at the time. Today, demi-glace, brown sauce and *Sauce Espagnole* are terms that are used interchangeably. The original basis for these names no longer applies and experts vary in their intepretation and use of these terms.

Meat glaze (*glace de viande***)** Further reduction of demi-glace produces a strengthening and flavouring agent called a meat glaze (or *glace de viande*). In domestic cooking excellent results can be achieved without going to this length.

Simple brown sauce Recipes calling for a brown sauce made by thickening brown stock with a brown roux achieve the consistency described above but obviously cannot match the flavour.

SAUCE BRUNE
Brown Sauce

A proper brown sauce starts out with a good brown stock. The sauce is developed by slow simmering for hours, thereby intensifying its flavour and changing its consistency. It is not really necessary to make a brown sauce of this grandeur for home use. The recipe that follows is very good and much simpler. It can be made ahead and frozen. I find it very handy to make some in advance and freeze it ready to use whenever I need it.

Cooking time: about 45 minutes
To make about 200 ml/7 fl oz/scant 1 cup

INGREDIENTS	METRIC	IMPERIAL	AMERICAN
Butter	25 g	1 oz	2 tbsp
Onion, carrot, celery, diced, together measuring	2 tbsp	2 tbsp	2 tbsp
Flour	15 g	½ oz	1 tbsp
Brown stock	275 ml	½ pt	1¼ cups
Tomato concentrate	5 ml	1 tsp	1 tsp
Mushroom trimmings	2 tsp	2 tsp	2 tsp
Bouquet garni (made with a few sprigs of thyme, parsley stalks and 1 bay leaf tied together with string)			
Salt and freshly ground black pepper to taste			

Hint *If you wish to make this recipe with tinned beef bouillon rather than making a brown stock, then the bouillon needs a little doctoring first. Add about 3 tablespoons of chopped carrots and onions, one tablespoon of chopped celery, 125 ml/4 fl oz/½ cup of red wine and a bouquet garni made of 1 bay leaf, a few sprigs of parsley and a sprig of thyme to a 425 ml/15 fl oz tin of bouillon. Simmer all the ingredients together for about half an hour and sieve. Use instead of the brown stock.*

Warm the butter in a heavy-bottomed saucepan. Add the vegetables and cook gently until they shrivel but do not colour. Add the flour and cook very slowly until a russet brown colour.

Hint *This may take several minutes and is a step that cannot be hurried. If you cook the flour too fast it will burn rather than turn brown and give the sauce a bitter, burned flavour.*

Cool the vegetables a little. Pour in the stock all at once, saving about 50 ml/2 fl oz/¼ cup for later. Stir until simmering. Add the tomato concentrate, mushrooms, and bouquet garni and simmer for 20–25 minutes with half a lid. Strain into a clean pan. Bring to the boil and add the reserved stock. Scum will come to the top as the sauce comes back to the boil. Skim it off. Taste for salt and pepper.

Opposite: *Vinaigrette au Vinaigre de Vin de Xérès* (page 22).

SAUCE TOMATE
Tomato Sauce

For meat, vegetables, fish, pasta or eggs

This is an all-purpose sauce that forms the base of many sauces and goes with many foods. It freezes beautifully, and I try to have several jars frozen to be used whenever I need them. The best time of year to make this sauce is in late summer and early autumn when the tomatoes are just coming into season and are full of flavour. Fresh tomatoes don't have much flavour in the winter season so it is best to use a good quality tinned tomato instead.

Cooking time: 1 hour   To serve 6

INGREDIENTS	METRIC	IMPERIAL	AMERICAN
Unsalted butter	25 g	1 oz	2 tbsp
Large onion, sliced	1	1	1
Clove garlic, crushed	1	1	1
Ripe plum tomatoes	900 g	2 lb	2 lb
OR Tinned tomatoes	680 g	1½ lb	4 cups
Bouquet garni (made with few sprigs of thyme or 1 tsp/5 g dried thyme, parsley stalks and 1 bay leaf)			
Tomato purée (optional)	10 ml	2 tsp	2 tsp
Sugar	1 tsp	1 tsp	1 tsp

Hint *The sugar helps to counteract the acidity of the tomatoes. Adding a sliced carrot or a few pieces of dried orange rind instead when cooking the onions can help.*

Salt and freshly ground black pepper to taste			

Melt the butter in a heavy-bottomed saucepan. Add the onions and sauté until transparent, about 10–15 minutes. Add the garlic and sauté for another minute. Quarter the tomatoes and add to the onions. Add the bouquet garni, cover and simmer for 15 minutes. Take off the lid and continue to simmer gently for 30 minutes, stirring occasionally. The sauce should be thick. If it is too thick add some water, or if too thin, leave to simmer for a little longer. Add the tomato purée if using winter tomatoes. They need extra flavour and colour. Strain. Taste for seasoning. Add sugar, salt and pepper as needed.

To serve Serve warm, or use as the base for other recipes.

Opposite: *Sauce Mayonnaise aux Anchois* (page 28). *Sauce Mayonnaise Verte* (page 29). *Sauce Mayonnaise à la Tomate* (page 30).

Les Sauces Vinaigrettes

VINAIGRETTE SAUCES

It is essential to have a basic vinaigrette sauce as part of your repertoire. There are many variations and it can be used in numerous ways. A vinaigrette is a mixture of vinegar or lemon juice, or a little of both, with oil, mustard (optional), and salt and pepper. The variations are infinite. There are many types of vinegar to choose from as well as different oils and flavoured mustards. In addition, various fresh herbs can be added, providing texture and garden freshness to your sauce. Choose the combination to suit the food to be served. You will find that a varied assortment of salads, meats and fish are complemented by vinaigrettes.

The interest in new light French cuisine has brought to our shops a complete range of wine-based vinegars. The most popular ones are sherry wine vinegar and raspberry wine vinegar. There are also champagne, peach, cherry, blueberry, blackberry, garlic, tarragon and fennel vinegars, and others too numerous to list. Some types are too acid, so be careful to buy the best quality. Other vinegar bases, such as cider vinegar can be equally successful. One superb vinegar I use is made from honey and cider. These flavours can be used to vary your basic vinaigrette. However, they can also be used to enhance the flavour of your cooked vegetables. Simply pour 15 ml/1 tablespoon over your vegetables when adding melted butter, salt and pepper. Or, to make a refreshing summer drink, add 5 ml/1 tsp of a fruit vinegar to a glass of ice water or fizzy water. Then add a few berries or slices of the fresh fruit used in the vinegar.

To go along with the variety of vinegars, there are many different types of oils available. Olive oil is a natural oil that needs no refining. Pure virgin oil is the best. It is obtained from the first pressing of the olives and is extracted without heat. Walnut oil has a strong nutty flavour and goes well with salads. Hazelnut oil also has a nutty flavour. Neither oil keeps well. Sunflower oil is light and thin and is used where a mild light oil is needed. Corn oil is another light oil, but is stronger than sunflower oil. I usually use a light corn or sunflower oil in my vinaigrette. However, to achieve a different flavour, I mix these oils with a first quality olive, walnut or hazelnut oil. The latter two are so rich and delicious on their own that they can be used on a salad without any mustard or vinegar. Simply make your fresh salad and add salt and pepper. Prepare each serving on a separate dish and pour a spoonful of walnut or hazelnut oil over the top.

The third ingredient in a basic vinaigrette is the mustard. This is an optional ingredient but one that can add intriguing flavours. I have recently tasted an orange mustard that is sensational on its own. There are also lemon, black olive, tarragon, herbed and armagnac mustards, and many others. A good quality dijon mustard is a common one used in a basic vinaigrette.

A point to remember when creating your own vinaigrettes: keep the sauces simple. If using a special type of oil, then use a plain vinegar and mustard. Or when using a special vinegar then a light oil is best. Let one interesting flavour dominate. Armed with this vast array to choose from, it can be fun and easy to develop vinaigrettes.

Making wine vinegar

I am often asked how I make my own wine vinegar. It is easy to make and adds a mellow flavour to my vinaigrettes. The results are worth the little bit of effort that is necessary. It is milder and less acidic than commercial varieties. Having once produced a good wine vinegar, I can add any type of flavour I choose.

Wine vinegar is the fermentation of wine under the action of a mould. This is called a *mère de vinaigre*, mother of vinegar. If wine is opened and left in a warm place between 15–30°C/59–85°F a thin white veil starts to appear. It eventually becomes heavy and sinks to the bottom of the wine forming a thick jelly-like substance. This is the mother.

It is quite simple to make the vinegar. Besides the wine, you need a mother of vinegar and a vinaigrier. The mother can be made by leaving wine in a vinaigrier (pot that holds wine vinegar) or other earthenware jug in warm weather as mentioned above. Or, it can be bought from some speciality food or kitchen equipment shops. Usually, it is passed from friend to friend. Once a mother has started, it produces babies that can then be used in other vinaigriers.

The storage jug or barrel can be made of wood or earthenware. (In Italy a glass jar is used, but the top remains open.) The storage pot needs to be a porous material so the vinegar can breathe. It should have a tap at the bottom of the jug so that the vinegar can be drawn off at the bottom while new wine or ends of bottles are poured in at the top.

To start a vinaigrier, place a mother in a clean vinaigrier. It is best to scald the vinaigrier with boiling water to be sure it is clean. Make sure it is cool when the mother is placed in it. Add about 175–225 ml/6–8 fl oz ¾–1 cup of wine. (Use either red or white wine, but do not mix the two. Pasteurised wine will not work.) Add about this quantity of wine every other day until the jug is half filled.

The vinegar should be left for about a month before being used. After this, wine should be added (feeding the mother) about 2–3 times a week. It should be kept away from direct sunlight and in a cool spot. The vinaigrier, properly cared for, can go on for years. I draw off a small jar full at a time and keep it handy for daily use. This is easier than taking it from the tap each time.

SAUCE VINAIGRETTE
French Dressing

The recipe below will give you a thick sauce with a creamy consistency. I prefer this to a vinaigrette that separates with the oil floating on top. If made in the food processor, it will produce a sauce almost as thick as a mayonnaise. It will keep for a few days in the refrigerator, but it only takes a few minutes to make and is best made fresh.

Preparation time: 5 minutes
To make about 225 ml/8 fl oz/1 cup

INGREDIENTS	METRIC	IMPERIAL	AMERICAN
Wine vinegar	30 ml	2 tbsp	2 tbsp

Hint *Use a good quality wine vinegar, or use lemon juice.*

Mustard	10 ml	2 tsp	2 tsp

Hint *I prefer a dijon mustard in my vinaigrettes. If you like a milder flavour, use a weaker mustard.*

Salt and freshly ground black pepper to taste (about ½ tsp)			
Oil	175 ml	6 fl oz	¾ cup

Hint *Use corn, sunflower, olive, walnut, hazelnut or any combination you wish.*

Whisk the vinegar and mustard together thoroughly. Be sure they are well mixed. Add salt and pepper to taste. Pour in the oil and whisk together. Taste for seasoning. It should be a creamy texture.

Hint *If your mixture separates, this means that the mustard and vinegar were not thoroughly blended before the oil was added.*

Sometimes you can bring it back together by processing it in a food processor with an ice cube. If it is too far gone for this trick, then start with more vinegar and mustard well mixed and slowly add the separated mixture. Adjust the seasoning.

VINAIGRETTE VERTE
Green Vinaigrette

To accompany cold meats

This thick, green herb sauce has the delightful smell of a fresh spring garden. The addition of chopped hard-boiled egg and lettuce leaves to a basic vinaigrette make this an interesting sauce that works well with cold meats. It is especially good with cold tongue.

Preparation time 10–15 minutes   To serve 6

INGREDIENTS	METRIC	IMPERIAL	AMERICAN
Hard-boiled egg	1	1	1
Lettuce leaves, washed and dried	3	3	3
Fresh parsley, washed and dried	50 g	2 oz	¼ cup
Red wine vinegar	90 ml	6 tbsp	6 tbsp
Light oil	175 ml	6 fl oz	¾ cup
Salt and freshly ground black pepper to taste			

Chop the egg, lettuce leaves and parsley together. Add the vinegar and oil. Mix well. Add salt and pepper and taste for seasoning.

To serve Serve in a sauce boat to accompany any cold meat.

MOULES VINAIGRETTE

Mussels in Vinaigrette Sauce

In most fishmongers, mussels are now being sold by the pound rather than by the pint or litre. It is really an easier way to judge how many you need. Spanish and Irish mussels are large, and if measured by the pint, might only give you 6. You should count on 225 g/½ lb per person for a first course and double that for a main course. This dish can easily be made in advance and used for a first course, main course or buffet.

Cooking time: 30 minutes   To serve 6

INGREDIENTS	METRIC	IMPERIAL	AMERICAN
Butter	25 g	1 oz	2 tbsp
Shallots, chopped	3	3	3
Mussels	225 g	½ lb	½ lb
FOR THE VINAIGRETTE			
Champagne vinegar	45 ml	3 tbsp	3 tbsp
Dijon mustard	15 ml	1 tbsp	1 tbsp
Light vegetable oil	90 ml	6 tbsp	6 tbsp
Salt and freshly ground black pepper to taste			
TO GARNISH			
Very small baby green beans	100 g	4 oz	1 cup
Several lettuce leaves			
Fresh parsley, chopped	2 tbsp	2 tbsp	2 tbsp

Melt the butter in a heavy-bottomed pan and add the shallots. Sauté until they are transparent. Meanwhile scrub the mussels and remove the 'beard' (hairs that connect them to rocks). Discard any that are open. Place in the pan with the shallots and cover. Raise the heat and shake the pan. In about 2–3 minutes all the mussels will have opened. Do not overcook or they will become tough. Discard any that do not open. Remove the mussels from their shells and leave to cool. Carefully strain the mussel juice through butter muslin or kitchen towel. Place back on the heat and reduce by one half to concentrate the flavour. Set aside.

To make the vinaigrette Mix the vinegar and mustard together thoroughly. Add the oil and whisk again. Add 30 ml/2 tbsp of the mussel juice. Add salt and pepper. Taste for seasoning. Add more salt, pepper or juice, if needed.

For the garnish Tip and tail the green beans. To blanch, bring a pan of water to the boil and add the beans. As soon as the water comes back to the boil, take off the heat and drain. Refresh in cold water. This will stop the cooking, keep them crisp and set the green colour.

To serve Spoon the sauce over the mussels and toss with the green beans. Place on a platter lined with lettuce leaves. Sprinkle with chopped parsley. Serve at room temperature.

VINAIGRETTE AU VINAIGRE DE VIN DE XERES

Sherry Wine Vinaigrette with Chicken and Mango Salad

For cold meats or fruit salads

The rich flavour of the sherry wine vinegar makes this an excellent sauce for cold meats or fruit salads. A mixture of chicken, ripe mangoes and salad greens make a tangy first course or luncheon dish.

Cooking time: 20 minutes   To serve 6

INREDIENTS	METRIC	IMPERIAL	AMERICAN
FOR THE VINAIGRETTE			
Sherry wine vinegar	45 ml	3 tbsp	3 tbsp
Dijon mustard	15 ml	1 tbsp	1 tbsp
Clove garlic, crushed	1	1	1
Spring onion, washed and sliced	1	1	1
Brown sugar	1 tsp	1 tsp	1 tsp
Light vegetable oil	90 ml	6 tbsp	6 tbsp
Salt and freshly ground black pepper to taste			
FOR THE SALAD			
Chicken breast, cooked	275 g	10 oz	10 oz
Ripe mangoes, peeled and sliced	2	2	2
Cos, batavia or crisp lettuce	1	1	1
Tomatoes	2	2	2
TO GARNISH			
Fresh coriander leaves, chopped	2 tbsp	2 tbsp	2 tbsp

To make the vinaigrette Whisk together the sherry wine vinegar and the mustard. Add all the other ingredients except the oil. Mix well. Add the oil and whisk. Taste for seasoning. Add more if necessary. It should be a delicate blend with a sweet and sour taste.

To make the salad Slice the chicken in strips about a finger's length.

Hint *To keep the chicken moist it is best to poach it gently in some chicken stock and let it cool in the stock. It also steams beautifully in a microwave. Place the chicken on a dish with some chicken stock. Cover it with plastic wrap and steam for 2–3 minutes following the timing for your type of microwave.*

Peel the mangoes and slice in strips to match the chicken. Wash and drain the lettuce leaves. Quarter the tomatoes.

To finish Place the lettuce leaves on a round serving plate. Arrange the chicken and mangoes in a circle like the petals of a flower radiating from the centre and alternating the colours. Place the tomatoes in the centre for colour. Pour the dressing over the ingredients. Just before serving sprinkle with chopped fresh coriander leaves.

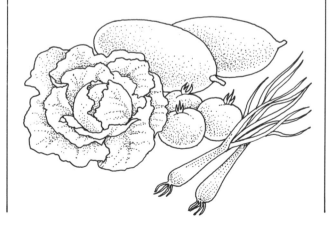

VINAIGRETTE A LA TOMATE

Tomato Vinaigrette with Avocado Salad

Ripe, green avocados served with a red tomato vinaigrette make a pretty and delicious dish. For the Christmas season make an avocado wreath with the red sauce to give your table a festive look.

Preparation time: 20 miniutes   To serve 6

INGREDIENTS	METRIC	IMPERIAL	AMERICAN
FOR THE VINAIGRETTE			
Red wine vinegar	60 ml	4 tbsp	¼ cup
Light vegetable oil	175 ml	6 fl oz	¾ cup
Tomato sauce (page 17)	275 ml	½ pt	1¼ cups
Salt and freshly ground black pepper to taste			
Chopped herbs (tarragon, parsley, chives, fresh if possible)	2 tbsp	2 tbsp	2 tbsp
FOR THE SALAD			
Avocados	3	3	3
Juice from lemons	2	2	2
Sticks of celery	4	4	4
Walnuts, broken in pieces	100 g	4 oz	1 cup
Shrimps or prawns	100 g	4 oz	1 cup

Add the vinegar and oil to the cool tomato sauce. Taste for seasoning. Add more salt, pepper or sugar as needed. If it needs more tartness, add a little lemon juice. Add the chopped herbs, saving a little back to sprinkle on top.

To finish Cut the avocados in half and remove the pits. Coat with lemon juice. Cut the celery into small bite-sized pieces. Mix the celery, walnuts and shrimps together. Spoon the tomato vinaigrette over them. Spoon into the centre of the avocado. Pour any extra sauce into a sauce boat.

The tomato sauce can be made several days ahead or made and frozen. The vinegar and oil can be added a day in advance. The salad is best cut a few hours before serving.

To serve Place each filled avocado on an individual plate and place on the table. Pass the sauce boat separately.

Hint *Avocado Wreath – Here is a variation for Christmas. Skin the avocados. Cut in half and take out the pit. Dip in lemon juice to help retain the green colour. Place some lettuce leaves on a round serving platter and put the avocados, rounded side up, in a circle around the platter. The narrow ends placed towards the centre. Spoon the tomato vinaigrette over the avocados and place a bouquet of watercress in the centre.*

SALADE DE HARICOTS VERTS

Garlic Vinaigrette with Green Bean and Red Onion Salad

A slight garlic flavour combined with a best quality olive oil make an excellent accompaniment to most vegetables. This green bean salad is a good example.

Preparation time: 15 minutes   To serve 6

INGREDIENTS	METRIC	IMPERIAL	AMERICAN
FOR THE VINAIGRETTE			
Garlic vinegar	45 ml	3 tbsp	3 tbsp
Dijon mustard	15 ml	1 tbsp	1 tbsp
Corn or sunflower oil	45 ml	3 tbsp	3 tbsp
Olive oil	45 ml	3 tbsp	3 tbsp
Salt and freshly ground black pepper to taste			
FOR THE SALAD			
Fresh small green beans	900 g	2 lb	2 lb
Red onions (if these onions are difficult to find, use chopped pimentoes for flavour and colour	2	2	2

Whisk the vinegar and mustard together. Add the corn or sunflower oil and mix well. Add the olive oil and whisk. Add salt and pepper to taste.

Tip and tail the beans. Place in a pan of boiling salted water. When the water comes back to the boil, cook for 1 minute and drain. Immediately pour cold water over them to stop the cooking and bring out their colour. Toss the beans in the vinaigrette. Lift them out and place in a shallow bowl or serving platter. Slice the onions so that they remain in circles. Place them in a pot of boiling salted water. As soon as the water comes back to the boil, drain the onions and refresh under cold water. Toss in the vinaigrette. Sprinkle the onions over the beans.

VINAIGRETTE AU PERSIL

Parsley Vinaigrette with Smoked Mackerel Salad

Fresh parsley can be bought year round. Its garden fresh taste and bright green colour add a special touch to a vinaigrette sauce. A fish salad of this type makes a light first course, luncheon dish or buffet dish.

Preparation time: 15 minutes   To serve 4–6

INGREDIENTS	METRIC	IMPERIAL	AMERICAN
FOR THE SAUCE			
Wine vinegar	30 ml	2 tbsp	2 tbsp
Dijon mustard	10 ml	2 tsp	2 tsp
Light oil (corn or sunflower)	90 ml	6 tbsp	6 tbsp
Fresh parsley, chopped	3 tbsp	3 tbsp	3 tbsp
Salt and freshly ground black pepper to taste			
FOR THE SALAD			
Smoked mackerel fillets	2	2	2
Medium onion	1	1	1
Dilled cucumbers or dilled pickles	2	2	2

Make the vinaigrette by whisking the vinegar and mustard together thoroughly and then adding the oil. Make sure the sauce is well mixed. Add half the parsley, and salt and pepper. Taste for seasoning and add more if necessary.

Skin the mackerel fillets and cut them into thick julienne strips (about 4 cm/1½ ins long). Cut the onion into rings. Bring a pot of water to the boil. Add the onion rings. When the water returns to the boil, drain the onions and rinse in cold water. Cut the dilled cucumbers into 6 mm/¼ in diagonals.

To serve Place the fish on a serving dish making sure all the fish has some vinaigrette spooned over it. Sprinkle the onions on the fish. Place a border of the dilled cucumbers around the edge. Sprinkle the remaining chopped parsley on top.

CROTTIN DE CHAVIGNOL MARINES AUX HERBES AROMATIQUES
Vinaigrette for Marinated Goat's Cheese

This is a vinaigrette that first imparts its flavour to the cheese and then becomes a delicious sauce on its own once the cheese has been used. *Chèvre* or goat's cheese is well known in France and is becoming more popular in England. The cheese absorbs the flavours of the marinade; and the vinaigrette with a slight *chèvre* flavour makes a wonderful salad dressing.

Preparation time: 10 minutes plus marinating time: 1 week
To serve 6

INGREDIENTS	METRIC	IMPERIAL	AMERICAN
First quality olive oil	425 ml	¾ pt	2 cups
Whole garlic cloves, unpeeled	4	4	4
Peppercorns	12	12	12
Bay leaf	1	1	
Sprig fresh thyme	1	1	1
Small dried red chilli peppers	2	2	
Coriander seeds	8	8	8
Crottin, montrachet or other small fairly dry goat cheese.			

Hint: *Farm produced cheese are best. They should be rindless. If choosing a larger goat cheese, then remove the rind and cut into large chunks.*

Place all the marinade ingredients in a wide-mouthed jar large enough to hold the cheese. Place the cheese in the jar. Add more oil to cover the cheese, if necessary. Cover and keep in a cool place. Leave for at least a week but no longer than a month. The cheese becomes too soft and the oil turns rancid after this.

To serve Serve with hot toast or biscuits. The cheese can also be placed on the grill and warmed until bubbly and browned. Baste with the oil while grilling.

To use the oil as a sauce for salads, strain and sprinkle on fresh vegetables.

25

Les Mayonnaises
MAYONNAISE SAUCES

Once a good mayonnaise sauce is mastered, many sauces can be built on it. Any number of different flavours can be obtained by the use of various flavoured mustards, fruit-flavoured vinegars or the use of different oils. Its fun to experiment and develop sauces to fit your tastes and needs. The recipes that follow will give you an idea of what types of sauces can be made. Recipe suggestions accompany each sauce to illustrate their various uses.

Mayonnaise is an emulsion. One fat, oil, is suspended in another, egg yolk. Certain rules must be followed in order to achieve the desired suspension. It is very simple to make, especially with an electric mixer or food processor, and will last for at least a week or more in the refrigerator. I find it tastes better than bought preparations. It has literally hundreds of uses as a mother sauce.

The recipe can be made by hand, or more quickly and easily in a food processor or with an electric beater. Mayonnaise which is made in a blender is based on a different recipe and has a different texture.

General rules
1 One egg yolk will accept about 150–175 g/5–6 fl oz/²/₃–³/₄ cup of oil. If too much oil is added the mixture will break down (curdle).
2 The egg yolk should be prepared to receive the oil. This is done by beating the yolk thoroughly before any oil is added.
3 The oil must be added to the yolk very slowly so that the yolk will be able to absorb the oil.
4 For the best results the egg yolk and oil should be at room temperature.

How to correct problems
If your mixture curdles, do not throw it away. Start with another egg yolk and add the curdled mixture drop by drop as you did for the oil.

SAUCE MAYONNAISE
— Mayonnaise —

Preparation time: 10 minutes
To make about 300 ml/½ pt/1¼ cups

INGREDIENTS	METRIC	IMPERIAL	AMERICAN
Egg yolk	2	2	2
Mustard	5 ml	1 tsp	1 tsp
Salt and freshly ground black pepper to taste			
Oil (corn, sunflower or olive)	300 ml	½ pt	1¼ cups
Wine vinegar or lemon juice	15 ml	1 tbsp	1 tbsp

Beat the egg yolks, add the mustard and add a little salt and pepper (about 1 tsp of salt). When the yolks are creamy, add the oil drop by drop, beating constantly. As the mayonnaise begins to thicken, the oil can be added at a faster pace. When nearly all the oil has been added, pour in the vinegar and finish with the remaining oil, beating constantly. Taste for salt and pepper.

To make in the food processor The method is the same as above, except the machine is doing the work for you and will do it faster. Add the egg yolks and mustard and process. With the machine running, add the oil through the feed tube little by little. Complete with the vinegar, salt and pepper as above.

Mayonnaise ideas

Here are some other mayonnaise ideas. They can all be used as accompaniments to cold meats, fish, crab or lobster, steamed vegetables or potatoes. Choose your favourite flavour and create your own dish.

An hors d'oeuvre or first course that most people love is crudités. Choose a flavoured mayonnaise. Hollow out a green or red cabbage and fill it with the mayonnaise. Select the best quality vegetables available such as baby mangetouts, asparagus, small green beans, cherry tomatoes, white radish or any others you might find in the market. Clean them and blanch the tougher ones. Arrange them attractively on a platter with the sauce in the centre.

SAUCE MAYONNAISE AU CRESSON
—Watercress Mayonnaise—

With the addition of fresh watercress and some cream to a basic mayonnaise, a tangy sauce results.

Preparation time: 15 minutes
To make about 400 ml/14 fl oz/1¾ cups

INGREDIENTS	METRIC	IMPERIAL	AMERICAN
Fresh watercress	2 bunches	2 bunches	2 bunches
Mayonnaise	275 ml	½ pt	1¼ cups
Whipping cream	125 ml	4 fl oz	½ cup
Salt and freshly ground white pepper to taste			

Carefully wash the watercress. Fill a sink with cold water and soak the watercress. Lift out of the water and dry. Take the leaves off the stems and plunge them into a pot of boiling salted water. As soon as the water comes back to the boil, drain the watercress and refresh with cold water. Dry the leaves thoroughly and purée or chop finely. This can be done in a food processor or blender. Add to the mayonnaise. Slightly whip the cream until it just holds its shape. Fold into the mayonnaise mixture. Taste for seasoning. Add salt and pepper if necessary.

SAUCE MAYONNAISE AU COGNAC
—Cognac Mayonnaise—

Preparation time: 15 minutes
To make about 350 ml/12 fl oz/1½ cups

INGREDIENTS	METRIC	IMPERIAL	AMERICAN
Tomato purée	15 ml	1 tbsp	1 tbsp
Cognac or armagnac	30 ml	2 tbsp	2 tbsp
Mayonnaise	275 ml	½ pt	1¼ cups

Add the tomato purée and cognac to the mayonnaise and mix well. Adjust seasoning if necessary.

SAUCE MAYONNAISE AUX ANCHOIS
Anchovy Mayonnaise

Preparation time: 15 minutes
To make about 275 ml/½ pt/1¼ cups

INGREDIENTS	METRIC	IMPERIAL	AMERICAN
Anchovy fillets, chopped	1 tbsp	1 tbsp	1 tbsp
Anchovy paste	15 ml	1 tbsp	1tbsp
Mayonnaise	275 ml	½ pt	1¼ cups

Add the anchovy fillets and paste to the mayonnaise and mix well. Taste for seasoning. Add more anchovy paste for a stronger flavour.

SAUCE MAYONNAISE A LA FRAMBOISE
Raspberry Mayonnaise

This recipe can be used with any type of fruity vinegar.

Preparation time: 10–15 minutes
To make about 350 ml/12 fl oz/1½ cups

INGREDIENTS	METRIC	IMPERIAL	AMERICAN
Raspberry vinegar	15 ml	1 tbsp	1 tbsp
Ingredients for mayonnaise to make	275 ml	½ pt	1¼ cups
Fresh raspberries, washed and drained	50 g	2 oz	¼ cup

Follow the basic recipe for making mayonnaise substituting the fruit vinegar for wine vinegar. Fold in the fresh raspberries.

Hint *The various brands of vinegars differ in intensity. You may have to add more or less according to your own palate.*

SAUCE MAYONNAISE SANS OEUFS
Mayonnaise without Eggs

This is a very useful recipe for those who for one reason or another cannot eat eggs. As you can see, this is a low cholesterol mayonnaise. The principle is to create an oil and water emulsion by having the ingredients very cold. It can be used just as ordinary mayonnaise.

Preparation time: 15 minutes
To make about 350 ml/12 fl oz/1½ cups

INGREDIENTS	METRIC	IMPERIAL	AMERICAN
Dijon mustard	45 ml	3 tbsp	3 tbsp
Good wine vinegar or lemon juice	30 ml	2 tbsp	2 tbsp
Ice water	30 ml	2 tbsp	2 tbsp
Oil (corn or sunflower, with about 50–85 ml/2–3 fl oz/¼–⅓ cup of olive oil if you have it)	225 ml	8 fl oz	1 cup
Cold skimmed milk or powdered skimmed milk	30 ml	2 tbsp	2 tbsp
Salt and freshly ground black pepper to taste			

In a food processor, blend the mustard, vinegar and water together. With the machine running, pour in the oil drop by drop. When the mixture starts to thicken you can pour the oil in faster. As it starts to thicken, alternate oil with milk. When finished it will be as thick as mayonnaise.

Hint *The ingredients should be very cold for the mixture to take hold. If they aren't, then use 2–3 ice cubes instead of cold water.*

Add salt and pepper. Store in a covered jar in the refrigerator. It will keep for at least a week.

SAUCE MAYONNAISE VERTE
— *Green Herb Mayonnaise* —

For cold poached fish

This is a very pretty mayonnaise variation. The fresh herbs not only give it an attractive green colour, they also give a fresh flavour. It goes very well with cold salmon, salmon trout or other poached fish served cold, and makes a pleasant change from the usual sauces for salmon.

Preparation time: 20 minutes   To serve 6

INGREDIENTS	METRIC	IMPERIAL	AMERICAN
Fresh spinach leaves, washed	10–12	10–12	10–12
Fresh parsley	4 tbsp	4 tbsp	4 tbsp
Fresh tarragon (use half the amount if using dried tarragon)	1 tbsp	1 tbsp	1 tbsp
Fresh watercress (leaves removed)	3–4 sprigs	3–4 sprigs	3–4 sprigs
Shallots	2	2	2
Mayonnaise	450 ml	16 fl oz	2 cups
Salt and freshly ground white pepper to taste			

Place all the greens and the shallots in a food processor and chop finely, or chop by hand on a board. Bring a saucepan of water to the boil and add the chopped ingredients. As soon as the water returns to the boil, strain and run the herbs under cold water. Strain carefully, and pat dry with kitchen towel.

Hint *If the herbs are wet they will water down your sauce.*

Add the herb mixture to the mayonnaise and taste for seasoning. Add more salt and pepper as needed.

This can be made 1–2 days in advance. If kept longer, it will lose some of its colour.

Variation: fresh herbed mayonnaise To achieve a crisp, fresher mayonnaise, omit the spinach and add fresh chives and basil (optional). Chop all the ingredients and mix into the mayonnaise without blanching. If made this way the herbs should be added to the mayonnaise on the day it is to be used. They will turn bitter if left for more than a day.

SAUCE MAYONNAISE A LA TOMATE

Tomato Mayonnaise with Mock Seafood Terrine

For cold fish, vegetables or meat

With the addition of fresh tomato juice, a simple mayonnaise is transformed into an attractive sauce that dresses up whatever dish it accompanies.

The mock terrine recipe that follows makes an elegant addition to any meal. I call this a mock terrine, because it is served like a terrine but the seafood is held together by aspic rather than a farce. To make your own aspic jelly is quite long and involved. Good quality aspic jelly powder is sold today. By adding a little white wine or madeira to the liquid aspic, a very good result can be achieved.

Preparation time: 1 hour   To serve 6

INGREDIENTS	METRIC	IMPERIAL	AMERICAN
FOR THE SAUCE			
Juice from tomatoes	6	6	6
Mayonnaise	425 ml	¾ pt	2 cups
FOR THE TERRINE			
Tomatoes	6	6	6
Aspic jelly powder to make	575 ml	1 pt	2½ cups
Dry white wine	125 ml	4 fl oz	½ cup
Shrimps or prawns, cooked and shelled (if possible use the large raw prawns usually found frozen, but shelled frozen shrimps can be used)	100 g	4 oz	1 cup
Chunks of crab meat (many fishmongers sell freshly cooked crab claws or good quality frozen or tinned crab can be used)	100 g	4 oz	1 cup
Fresh scallops	6	6	6

Hint *Any type of shellfish can be used. The important point to remember is that it should be fresh and of the finest quality.*

Loaf tin 8½" × 4½" × 2½"

Skin and seed the tomatoes. Place each tomato one at a time in boiling water. Leave for 10–12 seconds then place in cold water. The skin can then be removed quite easily. Cut the tomatoes into 6 wedges. Remove the seeds into a sieve and strain the juice into a bowl. Set aside the tomatoes. Add the juice to the mayonnaise and mix thoroughly. The mayonnaise should be pink and have a fresh tomato taste.

Hint *It is difficult to say how much actual juice you will obtain from the tomatoes; this* *really depends on the type of tomatoes and the season. If the mayonnaise does not have a strong enough tomato flavour, then either purée a tomato in a food processor and add this to the sauce or add a spoonful of tomato purée.*

To make the terrine Dissolve the aspic in water according to the packet instructions. Bring to the simmer, stirring constantly. As soon as little bubbles start to rise in the liquid take it off the heat and let it cool. Add the wine. It should be a syrupy consistency when ready to use.

To prepare the shrimps Defrost the shrimps and place them in a pot of boiling salted water. As soon as the water comes back to the boil remove the shrimps with a slotted spoon. Peel and cut into bite-sized pieces. (If using frozen shrimps that have been precooked then simply defrost them.)

To prepare the crab Try to buy very fresh crab that has been boiled that day. A good fishmonger will have them already cooked for you. Many sell just the crab claws. Remove the shells and cut the meat into pieces.

To prepare the scallops Ask the fishmonger to open the shells for you. Bring a pan of salted water to the boil and add the scallops. As soon as the water comes back to the boil, remove them. Slice into rounds.

To assemble the terrine Wet the loaf tin. Spoon about 6 mm/¼ in of aspic into the bottom of the tin.

> **Hint** *It is easier to work over ice water. Place the loaf tin in a roasting tin filled with ice cubes and water.*

When the aspic starts to gel, place a row of tomatoes down the centre lengthwise. The rounded tops should be towards the bottom. Spoon aspic over the tomatoes to keep them in place. Add the shellfish and the rest of the tomatoes in alternating layers, spooning aspic between each layer and waiting for it to almost gel before the next layer is added. Continue until the loaf tin is filled. The result will be the fish and tomatoes evenly spread throughout the loaf tin. Place in the refrigerator to set. This can be done a day in advance.

To serve When ready to serve, gently pull the aspic away from the sides of the tin. Dip the tin into tepid water and invert onto a serving platter. Decorate with watercress or parsley. Slice and serve with the tomato mayonnaise sauce.

SAUCE AÏOLI
Aïoli Sauce

For fish, snails, potatoes or hard-boiled eggs

Aïoli sauce is known in Provence as *beurre de Provence*. This is the part of France where nearly every restaurant serves a *soupe de poisson*, robust fish soup, with croûtons, *rouille* (a spicy garlic, tomato and saffron paste) and aïoli. It is a real treat. This sauce also goes well with poached fish, snails, cold boiled potatoes and hard-boiled eggs.

Preparation time: 15 minutes   To serve 6

INGREDIENTS	METRIC	IMPERIAL	AMERICAN
Egg yolk	1	1	1
Cloves garlic, crushed	2	2	2
Dijon mustard (or any mustard of your choice)	5 ml	1 tsp	1 tsp
Olive oil	150 ml	¼ pt	⅔ cup
Salt and freshly ground black pepper to taste			

This can be made by hand, in a food processor or with an electric beater. The principle is the same. Beat the egg yolk, garlic and mustard together until the yolk is slightly thickened. Add the oil drop by drop, beating constantly. When the mixture starts to resemble mayonnaise the oil can be added more quickly. Season.

Hint *This is a garlic-flavoured mayonnaise and can be made 2–3 days ahead.*

Store in a clean, covered jar in the refrigerator. To make it a coating sauce, add a little warm water. Mix well and add more water until the desired consistency is reached.

To serve Serve in a sauce boat, or as a coating for potatoes or eggs.

HORS D'OEUVRE A LA SAUCE AÏOLI
Aïoli Platter

As an unusual dish, try an aïoli platter. This makes a wonderful buffet platter or can be made on individual plates. Take a French round country loaf or *pain de seigle* (round rye bread), cut off the top and hollow out the centre.

Hint *Any firm round bread can be used.*

Fill the centre with the aïoli sauce and place in the middle of a large serving platter. Select various cooked meat, fish, eggs and vegetables to place around the sauce. Here are some ideas. Poach 900 g/1.4 kg/2–3 lb cod fillets. Cool in the poaching liquid. Roast a joint of beef fillet, keeping it as rare as possible. Cool and slice paper thin. Hard-boil several eggs, shell and cut in half. Blanch cauliflower florets, small French green beans, red and yellow peppers sliced in strips, and refresh in cold water. Drain. Boil small potatoes in their skins until tender. Peel. Open a tin of chick peas and drain. Other beans may be used. Prepare all the ingredients and place attractively round the platter. Decorate with sprigs of parsley or watercress.

Opposite: *Hors d'Oeuvre à la Sauce Aïoli* (page 32).
Overleaf: *Crevettes à la Sauce au Pernod* (page 40).

Les Sauces pour Poisson et Fruits de Mer

SAUCES FOR FISH

I find that more people now appreciate the flavour, texture and food value of fish. Although one can still encounter recipes that seem to say, 'fish is something to be endured', or that smother its delicate flavour by a rich sauce usually containing lots of cream and heavy spices. The secret to enjoying fish is its freshness. With fresh fish, beautifully cooked and served with a sauce equal to its delicate flavour and texture, you can almost sense and taste the sea.

Fish takes sauce beautifully. The delicate nature of a white fish combines well with a light white sauce. Many fish sauces develop from the liquid in which the fish is cooked, termed a court bouillon. There are also many sauces that can be prepared on their own and in advance. These can be warmed ready to serve when the fish is cooked. This is an advantage as fish takes very little cooking time and it is sometimes difficult to keep the fish warm, but not overdone, while the sauce is being finished. Fish must not be overcooked. It becomes dry and rubbery.

In this section, I have concentrated on the new light style in French cooking. It achieves its results by using fresh ingredients and thickening the liquid through reduction, and the addition of butter or a little cream. White Wine Sauce with Mustard, Red Wine Sauce, White Butter Sauce, Sorrel Sauce and Saffron Sauce are some examples of this type of sauce.

To provide some connection with tradition, I have included updated recipes for old favourites, examples of which are Hollandaise, Mousseline and Bercy Sauces.

There is an entire sea of fish to discover and enjoy. Take the plunge and see how easy it is to wave your whisk and create a fresh light dish in the current style.

Previous page: *Lotte à l'Orange* (page 42).
Opposite: *Sauce Portugaise aux Harengs* (page 46).

COURT BOUILLON

One of the most common methods of cooking fish is in a court bouillon. This is a seasoned and flavoured liquor. The bouillon is prepared in advance of poaching the fish. It can contain anything from lemon juice and pepper to an intricate combination of herbs, vegetables and wines. The recipe that follows is a very workable one. I have chosen ingredients that one usually has in the kitchen so that the liquid can easily be prepared.

The advantages of poaching fish in a court bouillon is that the fish remains moist as well as absorbing the flavours from the liquid. The fish should never be boiled, only simmered. The court bouillon can be kept, strained and re-used several times. It should be stored in the refrigerator and will keep for about 4–5 days. The liquid should barely cover the fish so alterations to the recipe should be made according to the type and size of the fish.

Cooking time: 30 minutes
To make 850 ml/1½ pts/3¾ cups

INGREDIENTS	METRIC	IMPERIAL	AMERICAN
Water	575 ml	1 pt	2½ cups
White wine	275 ml	½ pt	1¼ cups
Juice of lemon	½	½	½
OR Vinegar	15 ml	1 tbsp	1 tbsp
Carrots, sliced	2	2	2
Large onion, peeled and sliced	1	1	1
Peppercorns	6	6	6
Bouquet garni (made of parsley stalks, 1 bay leaf, sprigs of thyme)			

Place all the ingredients into a pot large enough to hold the fish to be cooked. Bring to the simmer and let cook gently for 30 minutes. This can be done well ahead of time. When you are ready to poach the fish, bring the bouillon to the simmer and add the fish.

SAUCE BERCY
Bercy Sauce

For fish fillets: sole, haddock, halibut or plaice

Sauce Bercy is one of the simplest of basic fish sauces. It is based on a blend of white wine and fish stock and can be made ahead and gently rewarmed when needed.

Cooking time 20–25 minutes   To serve 6

INGREDIENTS	METRIC	IMPERIAL	AMERICAN
Butter	25 g	1 oz	2 tbsp
Shallot, finely chopped	1	1	1
Dry white wine	175 ml	6 fl oz	¾ cup
Fish stock (page 14)	850 ml	1½ pt	3¾ cups
TO FINISH			
Unsalted butter	40 g	1½ oz	3 tbsp
Plain flour	25 g	1 oz	¼ cup
Salt and freshly ground white pepper to taste			
Unsalted butter	50 g	2 oz	¼ cup
Fresh parsley, chopped	1 tbsp	1 tbsp	1 tbsp

Melt the butter in a saucepan and sauté the shallots until they are transparent. Add the wine and 175 ml/6 fl oz/¾ cup of fish stock. Let the liquid boil and reduce by one half. Add the remaining stock and boil for 10 minutes.

Make the beurre manie by blending the butter and flour together with a fork to make a paste. Whisk into the sauce little by little over a low heat. The sauce will thicken as it cooks. Season. Just before serving stir in the 2 oz butter (optional) and sprinkle the chopped parsley on top of the sauce.

To serve Serve hot spooned over any poached or grilled fish.

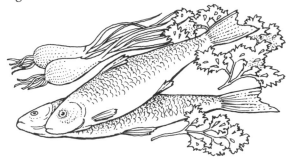

Sauce au Vin Blanc et aux Grains de Moutarde

White Wine Sauce with Mustard

For any white fish that has been poached in a court bouillon

The secret of this sauce is its simplicity. A very light and delicate sauce makes the best accompaniment to really fresh fish which has been delicately poached.

I usually find that keeping a poached fish warm while a sauce is being made somewhat difficult. The following sauce can be made in advance using a fish stock that has been reduced to concentrate the flavour. Thus, the sauce can be ready at the same time as the fish.

Cooking time: 30 minutes   To serve 6

INGREDIENTS	METRIC	IMPERIAL	AMERICAN
Fish stock (page 14)	450 ml	16 fl oz	2 cups
Tomatoes, peeled and seeded	3	3	3
Coarse grained mustard (moutarde de meaux)	30 ml	2 tbsp	2 tbsp
Unsalted butter	50 g	2 oz	¼ cup
Dry white wine	50 ml	2 fl oz	¼ cup
Salt and freshly ground white pepper to taste			

Reduce the fish stock by about one half. Strain. Dice the tomatoes and add them with the mustard to the sauce. Add the butter and white wine. Gently simmer to heat through. Do not overheat. The tomatoes should be only just warmed through. Their fresh taste gives the sauce its delicate flavour. Season with salt and pepper.

Poach whatever fish you choose in a court bouillon. Remove the fish to a warm platter.

To serve Spoon the sauce over the poached fish and serve immediately.

Hint *Should you wish to make this recipe and not have any fish stock, poach the fish in a court bouillon. When it is finished, remove to a warm platter and cover to keep warm. Turn the heat to high and reduce the court bouillon to 225 ml/8 fl oz/1 cup and proceed to make the sauce as above.*

35

SAUCE AU VIN ROUGE
Red Wine Sauce

For any type of poached fish or quenelles

By gently heating egg yolks and whisking in red wine and stock, an airy, light sabayon type of sauce is created. The sauce can easily be made while the fish is poaching.

Cooking time: 25 minutes   To serve 6

INGREDIENTS	METRIC	IMPERIAL	AMERICAN
Red wine (a good bordeaux)	125 ml	4 fl oz	½ cup
Concentrated fish stock	125 ml	4 fl oz	½ cup
Egg yolks	4	4	4
Cold water	175 ml	6 fl oz	¾ cup
A little freshly ground black pepper			

Place the wine and stock in a small saucepan and bring to the boil. Reduce by one half. Meanwhile whisk the yolks and water with a wire whisk until the mixture becomes thick and foamy. Without heat, rapidly whisk the egg yolk mixture into the reduced wine and stock. Place the saucepan over a low heat and gently cook, whisking all the time, until the yolks set. Be careful not to overheat the sauce or the yolks will curdle. Add pepper to taste.

Hint *It may take as long as 10 minutes to slowly thicken the sauce. Try not to hurry this process.*

The sauce can be kept warm by leaving it in a bain marie filled with hot water. When ready to use, very gently heat the water while constantly stirring the sauce.

To serve Spoon the sauce over the fish and serve.

———— *By way of explanation* ————

Hollandaise is an example of a group of sauces that depend on an emulsion of egg yolks and butter instead of flour and butter to give them their body. The Bernaise and Mousseline recipes that follow are other examples.

Beurre Blanc or white butter sauce is related. It is, in fact, a suspension of butter in vinegar.

SAUCE HOLLANDAISE
Hollandaise Sauce

For fish, vegetables or eggs

Hollandaise Sauce is one of the most famous of French sauces. It is also one that is often avoided at home because of its tendency to break down or curdle. One way to overcome a fear of making a last minute sauce is to make it in a liquidiser or food processor. This takes only seconds and is almost always successful. I have given a recipe for both the traditional and processor methods.

Cooking time: 25 minutes   To serve 6

INGREDIENTS	METRIC	IMPERIAL	AMERICAN
White wine vinegar	90 ml	6 tbsp	6 tbsp
Peppercorns	8	8	8
Bay leaf	1	1	1
Slice of onion	1	1	1
Blades of mace (the outer covering of nutmeg) (optional)	2	2	2
Egg yolks	3	3	3
Soft, unsalted butter, cut into cubes	175 g	6 oz	¾ cup
Salt and freshly ground white pepper to taste			
A few drops of lemon juice (optional)			

Hints *There are two main points to remember. The egg yolks must be warmed very gently. If the heat is too high they will curdle. The second point is that the yolks can only absorb the butter slowly. If too much butter is added at one time the sauce will not thicken.*

Place the vinegar, peppercorns, bay leaf, onion and blades of mace into a small heavy-bottomed saucepan. Bring to the boil and reduce to about 30 ml/2 tbsp. Strain and set aside. Place the egg yolks in the saucepan and place in a bain marie over a low heat. Whisk to warm the eggs. Add the reduced vinegar. Whisking constantly, add a cube of butter. As this is absorbed add another nut of butter. Continue slowly in this way until all the butter is absorbed.

Hint *It is a good idea to test the water of the bain marie with your finger. If the water is hot to the touch, then take the pan out and wait for the water to cool.*

Once the sauce has thickened, take off the heat and continue to whisk until it has cooled. Taste for seasoning and add more if necessary. If a sharper flavour is desired, add a few drops of lemon juice.

The sauce can be made 1–2 hours in advance and kept warm in a bain marie filled with warm water. When needed, simply raise the heat and whisk constantly until the sauce is warmed through.

To serve Pour into a sauce boat and serve warm with poached fish.

Hints for hollandaise

If the sauce starts to curdle or separate, take it off the heat and put an ice cube in it, stirring constantly. If it is already too badly curdled, this trick won't work. Use the following method.

If the sauce will not thicken, warm a small mixing bowl by running hot water over the back of the bowl. Add 5 ml/1 tsp lemon juice to the bowl. Beat in 15 ml/1 tbsp of sauce with a whisk. When this mixture thickens, add another spoonful of the sauce. Continue until all the sauce has been thickened.

If the sauce is too thick, whisk in 30 ml/2 tbsp of hot water.

SAUCE HOLLANDAISE 2

Food Processor Hollandaise Sauce

By using this quick method, a hollandaise can be easily made a few minutes before it is needed. The principle is the same as for traditional hollandaise. The egg yolks are flavoured with infused wine vinegar and are prepared to absorb the butter. The butter in this instance is heated in order to gently warm the yolks.

Cooking time: 5 minutes   To serve 6

INGREDIENTS	METRIC	IMPERIAL	AMERICAN
White wine vinegar	90 ml	6 tbsp	6 tbsp
Peppercorns	8	8	8
Bay leaf	1	1	1
Slice of onion	1	1	1
Blades of mace (the outer covering of the nutmeg) (optional)	2	2	2
Egg yolks	3	3	3
Unsalted butter, very soft	175 g	6 oz	¾ cup
Salt and freshly ground white pepper to taste			
A few drops of lemon juice (optional)			

Place the white wine vinegar, peppercorns, bay leaf, slice of onion and blade of mace in a small saucepan. Bring the liquid to the boil and reduce to about 30 ml/2 tbsp. Place the egg yolks in the bowl of a food processor fitted with a metal blade. With the motor running strain the vinegar into the egg yolks. Melt the butter until it is foaming but not burning. With the motor running, very slowly pour the butter into the yolks.

Watch the mixture to be sure it is thickening. Stop pouring and let the machine run for a few seconds if it looks too thin. Taste for seasoning and add salt and pepper as necessary. If a sharper flavour is desired, add a few drops of lemon juice.

Hint *The warmed butter is the only cooking the sauce has. Try to get the butter very hot, but pour it slowly so as not to burn or curdle the egg yolks.*

To serve Pour into a sauce boat and serve immediately with poached fish.

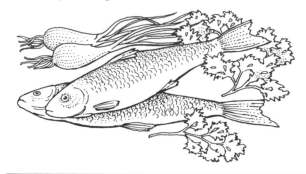

SAUCE MOUSSELINE

Mousseline Sauce

For fish, soufflés, asparagus

Folding chilled whipped cream into a hollandaise just before it is served lightens the sauce.

Cooking time: 30 minutes   To serve 6

INGREDIENTS	METRIC	IMPERIAL	AMERICAN
Hollandaise sauce	425 ml	¾ pt	2 cups
Double or whipping cream	150 ml	¼ pt	⅔ cup

Beat the cream until stiff. Fold into the hollandaise when ready to serve.

BEURRE BLANC
White Butter Sauce

For poached or grilled fish, shellfish, asparagus or leeks

To my mind this is one of the finest of all French sauces. One of my favourite restaurants in Paris became famous for its *Beurre Blanc*. People would come there just for this delicate sauce. The light blend of flavours makes it a perfect companion to any fish poached in a court bouillon or grilled.

Although this sauce has been part of the French repertoire for over a hundred years, it fits beautifully with the new trend which emphasises light sauces that are not thickened with flour, but by careful blending of ingredients. Because it needs to be made just before serving, people shy away from making it at home. I find, however, that when my students taste it, they agree it is more than worth the effort. Try it and decide for yourself.

Cooking time: 25–30 minutes   To serve 6

INGREDIENTS	METRIC	IMPERIAL	AMERICAN
Shallots, finely chopped	2	2	2
White wine vinegar	90 ml	6 tbsp	6 tbsp
Dry white wine	90 ml	6 tbsp	6 tbsp
Salt	½ tsp	½ tsp	½ tsp
Large pinch freshly ground white pepper			
Unsalted butter, very cold	250 g	9 oz	1 cup + 1 tbsp

Place all the ingredients except the butter in a small heavy-bottomed saucepan. Bring the liquid to the boil and reduce until about 30 ml/ 2 tbsp remains. This is usually just enough to cover the bottom of the pan. Strain the liquid and pour back into the pan. This can be done in advance.

Cut the butter into little cubes. With a low heat under the pan, whisk in one piece of butter. Continue to whisk until it is completely dissolved. Add another piece. Do not add more butter until the previous piece has dissolved. Continue in this manner, stirring constantly over a low heat. The sauce will start to thicken and have the consistency of cream. Season with more salt and white pepper if necessary.

The sauce can be made 1–2 hours before needed. Reheat it by placing it over a pan of hot water and whisking it all the time. This can be tricky and it may break down.

To serve Pour into a sauce boat and serve immediately.

Hint *One restaurant once told me that they make their* Beurre Blanc *in advance and reheat it by pouring some boiling water into the sauce. I must admit, though, that the sauce tasted somewhat watered down.*

BARBUE AU BEURRE BLANC
──── Brill in White Butter Sauce ────

Brill, *barbue*, is a light-textured non-oily fish that to my mind far surpasses salmon or sole for delicacy and flavour. It is the perfect accompaniment to a fine *Beurre Blanc* sauce, although any non-oily fish can be used.

Cooking time: 30–45 minutes   To serve 6

INGREDIENTS	METRIC	IMPERIAL	AMERICAN
Brill (one whole fish will serve 6) fish fillets about 175 g/6 oz each	6	6	6
Court bouillon, enough to cover the fish	1.1 l	2 pts	5 cups

Heat the oven to 170°C/325°F/gas mark 3. Place the fish in a baking dish and cover with the court bouillon. Cover with a lid or foil. Place in the oven and poach for 30–45 minutes depending on the size of the fish. Fillets will take a shorter time. The fish is done when a curd forms on the surface of the court bouillon and the fish looks opaque rather than translucent. Do not over-cook the fish.

Hint *The fish can be placed in a saucepan with the court bouillon and slowly simmered on a hob rather than in the oven.*

Remove the fish from the dish, remove the bones and divide into six servings.

To serve Serve with the warm sauce.

SAUCE AU PERNOD
──── Pernod Sauce with Prawns ────
For shrimps, prawns, lobster or crab

The French love to sit in their cafés sipping a Pernod or Ricard and absorb the world as it goes by. These anise flavoured liquors are a very popular aperitif. I find this flavouring excellent for shellfish, providing a somewhat exotic taste. The sauce develops from cooking the fish. Substitute whatever other shellfish you like.

Cooking time: 25 minutes   To serve 6

INGREDIENTS	METRIC	IMPERIAL	AMERICAN
Prawns (it is difficult to find fresh ones. The large Pacific prawns are sold frozen and are quite good)	900 g	2 lb	2 lb
Unsalted butter	50 g	2 oz	¼ cup
Shallots, finely chopped	3	3	3
Small bulb fresh fennel, chopped	½	½	½
Pernod or Ricard (any anise flavoured liqueur may be used)	60 ml	4 tbsp	4 tbsp
Dry white wine	125 ml	4 fl oz	½ cup
Crème fraiche or double cream	225 ml	8 fl oz	1 cup
A few fresh tarragon leaves, chopped (optional)			
Salt and freshly ground white pepper to taste			

Peel the prawns and make a slit down the back where the black vein lies. Wash them under cold water and remove the vein. Drain. Place the butter in a frying pan and add the shallots and fennel. Sauté for 5 minutes. Add the prawns and sauté for another minute, tossing them in the pan. Pour in the Pernod and flambé.

Hint *To flambé, as soon as the Pernod is hot tip the pan and let the liqueur catch the gas flame. If using an electric hob, throw in a lighted match and remove it when the flames have died down.*

Add the wine and let the prawns simmer for 2–3 minutes. Remove the prawns with a slotted spoon. Keep them on a warm dish, covered to keep warm. Raise the heat and reduce the juices in the pan by half. The recipe can be made ahead to this point.

To finish Add the cream and cook for 1 minute. Return the prawns to the pan to warm through. Sprinkle the tarragon leaves over the sauce and season with salt and pepper to taste. Serve immediately.

SAUCE A L'OSEILLE
Sorrel Sauce

For fish: salmon, turbot, sole or brill are best

Sorrel, *l'oseille*, has a lemony flavour which lends itself beautifully to serving with fish. It looks very similar to spinach, but differs not only in flavour but in texture. When heated it melts to nearly a paste.
I can never resist a well-prepared sorrel sauce.

The original dish, *St Pierre à l'Oseille*, can be found in Normandy. *Saumon à l'Oseille* has become even more popular throughout France. I found a source near my country home where my friends grow sorrel and use it in eggs or soup.
Sorrel can be difficult to find outside city centres. I grow my own and freeze it in plastic bags for winter use. It can now be bought bottled, preserved in vinegar.

Cooking time: 15–20 minutes   To serve 6

INGREDIENTS	METRIC	IMPERIAL	AMERICAN
Fish stock	175 ml	6 fl oz	¾ cup
Dry vermouth	45 ml	3 tbsp	3 tbsp
Dry white wine	90 ml	6 tbsp	6 tbsp
Shallots, finely chopped	2	2	2
Sorrel	75 g	3 oz	3 oz
Double cream	275 ml	½ pt	1¼ cups
Unsalted butter	40 g	1½ oz	3 tbsp
Juice from lemon	½	½	½
Salt and freshly ground white pepper to taste			

Place the stock, vermouth, wine and shallots in a small saucepan and bring to the boil. Let it reduce until it is syrupy. Meanwhile wash the sorrel and remove the central rib. Slice thinly. When the sauce has reduced, add the cream and allow to simmer until the sauce is reduced. Add the sorrel and cook for 30 seconds. Remove the pan from the heat and stir in the butter with a wooden spoon. A whisk will break up the sorrel leaves. Add 2–3 drops of lemon juice and salt and pepper to taste. The sauce can be made in advance and gently rewarmed in a bain marie.

To serve Spoon some sauce over the fish and serve the rest in a sauce boat.

SAUCE AU SAFRAN
Saffron Sauce

For scallops, mussels or monk fish

Saffron is the dried stigma of a crocus flower (*Crocus sativus*). It must be painstakingly gathered by hand, and it may take as many as 75,000 flowers to produce 450 g/1 lb. No wonder it is expensive. However, it has always been so. In Taillevent's day (fourteenth century) a small quantity could cost as much as a horse. Fortunately, the flavour is so pungent that most recipes call for only a few threads of saffron. These threads, together with fish stock, white wine and cream, form an elegant accompaniment to shellfish.

Cooking time: 25 minutes   To serve 6

INGREDIENTS	METRIC	IMPERIAL	AMERICAN
Unsalted butter	25 g	1 oz	2 tbsp
Shallots, chopped	2	2	2
Fish stock (page 14)	175 ml	6 fl oz	¾ cup
Dry white wine	175 ml	6 fl oz	¾ cup
A few strands of saffron			
Boiling water	30 ml	2 tbsp	2 tbsp
Crème fraiche or double cream	425 ml	¾ pt	2 cups
Salt and freshly ground white pepper to taste			
Fresh parsley, chopped	1 tbsp	1 tbsp	1 tbsp

Melt the butter in a saucepan and sauté the shallots until transparent. Pour in the stock and wine. Bring to the boil and reduce by one half. Pour the boiling water over the saffron threads. Leave to steep for a few minutes, then add to the pan with the cream. Reduce by one half again. Season with salt and pepper. The sauce can be made a few hours in advance and gently rewarmed. Just before serving sprinkle on the parsley.

To serve Spoon the sauce over whatever fish you have poached and serve immediately.

LOTTE A L'ORANGE
Monk Fish in Orange Sauce

For monk fish, lotte, any firm-fleshed fish, or shellfish

Monk fish has now taken a well deserved place in haute cuisine. A few years ago it was hardly ever mentioned. It is a firm-fleshed fish very similar in texture to lobster or shrimp. Its one bone down the centre means there are no small bones to deal with. It goes well with this intriguing sauce of fennel, tomatoes, orange and lemon zest, and orange liqueur. It can be made in advance and rewarmed.

Cooking time: 25 minutes   To serve 6

INGREDIENTS	METRIC	IMPERIAL	AMERICAN
Unsalted butter	25 g	1 oz	2 tbsp
Monk fish, skinned, bone removed and cut into 5 cm/2 in cubes	600 g	1½ lb	1½ lb

Hint *Buy 175 g/6 oz per person if on the bone, or 100 g/4 oz per person if filleted.*

Large bulb of fennel cut into julienne or matchsticks	1	1	1
Stick of celery, cut into julienne or matchsticks	1	1	1
Carrots, cut into julienne or matchsticks	100 g	4 oz	4 oz
Orange liqueur (Cointreau, Grand Marnier, Triple Sec, Curaçao)	60 ml	4 tbsp	4 tbsp
Dry white wine	175 ml	6 fl oz	¾ cup
Tomato sauce (page 17)	175 ml	6 fl oz	¾ cup
Zest of orange	1	1	1
Zest of lemon	1	1	1
Salt and freshly ground black pepper to taste			
Pinch of sugar			
Potato flour (or cornflour)	1 tsp	1 tsp	1 tsp
Double cream	30 ml	2 tbsp	2 tbsp

Heat the butter in a heavy-bottomed casserole dish. Add the monk fish and brown all the pieces. Remove the fish and add the julienne vegetables. Sauté for 2–3 minutes. Return the fish to the casserole and add the liqueur and flambé.

Hint *To flambé, as soon as the liqueur is hot tip the pan and let it catch the gas flame.*

If using an electric hob, throw in a lighted match and remove it when the flames have died down.

Add the wine and tomato sauce.

Hint *If preparing the dish in advance, remove the fish at this stage and finish the sauce. When ready to serve, replace the fish and cook for 5–10 minutes.*

Cover and cook for about 5–10 minutes. Do not overcook the fish. It is done when it no longer looks transparent. Add the orange and lemon zest. Add salt and pepper and taste for seasoning. Due to the acid in the tomatoes and wine, you may need to add a pinch of sugar.

To finish Just before serving, mix the potato flour with the cream and add to the sauce. Bring the sauce to the simmer and adjust the seasoning.

To serve Serve warm as a first course or main course.

MOULES A LA NORMANDE
— *Mussels in Normandy Sauce* —
For mussels, clams or cockles

Mussels always remind me of the fresh sea air and lots of sunshine. Calvados and fresh cream give this recipe its Normandy name, a region where one can sit by the sea and enjoy mussels by the bowl full.

Cooking time: 20 minutes   To serve 6–8

INGREDIENTS	METRIC	IMPERIAL	AMERICAN
Mussels	2.7 kg	6 lb	6 lb

Hint *Mussels are now being sold by the pound rather than the pint or litre. For a first course count 225 g/½ lb per person. For a main course count 450 g/1 lb per person.*

Unsalted butter	50 g	2 oz	¼ cup
Large onions, sliced	2	2	2
Carrots, quartered	2	2	2
Sticks of celery, quartered	2	2	2
Dry white wine	350 ml	12 fl oz	1½ cups
Calvados (apple brandy)	50 ml	2 fl oz	¼ cup
Freshly ground black pepper to taste			
Crème fraiche or double cream	125 ml	4 fl oz	½ cup
Fresh parsley, chopped	175 g	6 oz	6 oz

To prepare the mussels Wash the mussels carefully under cold water. Scrape off the beard or thin hairs along the shell. This is how the mussel attaches itself to rocks. The mussels should be clean, but you will not be able to scrape off every barnacle and this is not necessary. If any mussels are open, tap them gently. Discard any that do not close.

To prepare the sauce Melt the butter in a large saucepan. Sauté the onions, carrots and celery until they start to shrivel but not colour. This may take 10 minutes. The recipe can be made ahead to this point. Add the white wine, Calvados and some freshly ground pepper. Add the mussels and cover tightly. Bring the liquid to the boil. Let boil for about 1 minute. The wine will boil up over the mussels and they will open. As soon as they are open, take off the heat. Do not overcook. The mussels will taste like rubber if you do. Discard any mussels that do not open.

To finish With a slotted spoon, lift the mussels out of the pan and place in a large serving bowl. Bring the liquid to the boil and reduce rapidly by half. Add the *crème fraiche*. Strain the sauce through a kitchen towel or butter muslin and pour over the mussels.

To serve Sprinkle with the chopped parsley and serve immediately.

HOMARD A L'ARMORICAINE

— *Lobster Armoricaine* —

For lobster, crayfish (crevette) or monk fish

You may find this sauce on menus as 'l'Americaine', leading people to believe it has American connections. Others feel that l'amoricaine is named after the ancient province of Armorique in Brittany. Whichever name you use, this is a highly flavoured sauce that is made from cooking a lobster cut into pieces, flambéing it in cognac and adding wine, tomatoes and herbs.

Although live lobsters are best for this recipe, frozen lobster or lobster tails, or crayfish can be used. I sometimes substitute monk fish for the lobster. It has a firm flesh similar to that of a lobster, is easier to find and more economical.

Cooking time: 25 minutes   To serve 6

INGREDIENTS	METRIC	IMPERIAL	AMERICAN
Live lobsters, each weighing about 700 g/1½ lb	3	3	3
Oil	30 ml	2 tbsp	2 tbsp
Onions, finely sliced	4	4	4
Cognac	50 ml	2 fl oz	¼ cup
Dry white wine (or enough to cover the lobster while it cooks)	425 ml	¾ pt	2 cups
Tomato purée	60 ml	4 tbsp	4 tbsp
Clove garlic, crushed	1	1	1
Large pinch cayenne powder			
Salt and freshly ground black pepper to taste			

TO GARNISH			
Fresh tarragon, chopped (if using dried use half the amount)	½ tsp	½ tsp	½ tsp
Fresh chervil, chopped, if available	½ tsp	½ tsp	½ tsp
Fresh parsley, chopped	1 tbsp	1 tbsp	1 tbsp

Cut the lobsters in two lengthwise. Separate the tails from the main body. Cut them into 4 pieces. Remove the claws and break at the joints. Pour the oil into a large heavy-bottomed casserole dish. Add the lobster and sauté until the shells become red. Remove the lobster and add the onions. Sauté until transparent. Return the lobster to the pan and add the cognac and flambé.

Hint *To flambé, heat the liquid and tip the pan so that the flames will light the cognac. If using an electric hob, throw in a lighted match and remove it when the flames have died down.*

Pour in the white wine and add the tomato purée, garlic, cayenne, salt and pepper. Bring the liquid to a simmer, cover and gently cook for 20 minutes. Taste for seasoning. Add more salt, pepper and cayenne if necessary. This can be made in advance and gently rewarmed when needed.

To serve Remove the lobster pieces to a serving dish and spoon the sauce over them. Sprinkle with the herbs just before serving.

SAUCE PORTUGAISE
—*Spicy Tomato and Pepper Sauce*—

For oily fish such as herring, mackerel, sardines, pilchards or sword fish

The hot chilli peppers give this sauce a spicy flavour. It's a wonderfully quick recipe because it can be made in advance and kept in the refrigerator for 2–3 days. When needed simply place the fish in a baking tin and pour the sauce over it. Cover and bake. A quick recipe follows the sauce recipe.

Cooking time: 25 minutes   To serve 6

INGREDIENTS	METRIC	IMPERIAL	AMERICAN
Olive oil	50 ml	2 fl oz	¼ cup
Medium onion, finely sliced	1	1	1
Small clove garlic, crushed	1	1	1
Dried red chilli peppers	½ tsp	½ tsp	½ tsp
Ripe tomatoes (for a finer sauce, peel and seed)	4	4	4
Bay leaf	1	1	1
Dry red wine	50 ml	2 fl oz	¼ cup
Salt and freshly ground black pepper to taste			

Pour the oil into a medium-sized saucepan. Add the onion and sauté gently until transparent. This may take 10 minutes. Add the garlic and chilli peppers and sauté for another minute. Quarter the tomatoes and add to the saucepan with the bay leaf and wine. Cover the pan and gently simmer for about 10 minutes. Stir the sauce to keep it from sticking to the bottom of the pan. Simmer until the tomatoes have cooked to a sauce consistency.

Hint *If the sauce looks a little watery, simmer it without a lid until it thickens.*

Taste for seasoning and add salt and pepper as necessary. Remove the bay leaf. Set the sauce aside or store in a clean jar in the refrigerator.
To serve May be served as a hot or cold dish.

SAUCE PORTUGAISE AUX HARENGS
—*Portugaise Sauce with Herrings*—

Any oily fish can be used with this sauce

Cooking time: 30 minutes   To serve 6

INGREDIENTS	METRIC	IMPERIAL	AMERICAN
Olive oil	15 ml	1 tbsp	1 tbsp
Herring, each weighing about 225 g/ ½ lb	6	6	6
Salt and freshly ground black pepper to taste			
Sauce Portugaise for 6 (left)			

Heat the oven to 230°C/450°F/gas mark 8. Oil a baking tin or ovenproof serving dish large enough to hold the herring in one layer. Place the fish in the tin and salt and pepper them. Pour the sauce over the fish and cover with a lid or foil. Place in the oven and bake for 30 minutes. Remove the cover and place under the grill for a few minutes to crisp the fish skin.

To serve Serve hot, making sure that each portion is served with some sauce. This dish can also be served cold.

SAUCE AUX MORILLES
Morel Sauce

For sole, any poached or grilled fish, or chicken

Morels, *morilles*, are a fungus or type of wild mushroom found in the spring in wooded areas. The best are little black pointed ones found in the mountains. They bring their wild, country flavour to this sauce making it a treat to serve. Dried or preserved morels are readily available in speciality shops and they work very well for this sauce.

Cooking time: 10 minutes   To serve 6

INGREDIENTS	METRIC	IMPERIAL	AMERICAN
FOR THE MUSHROOMS			
Unsalted butter	75 g	3 oz	⅓ cup
Medium onion, thinly sliced	1	1	1
Fresh morels, washed and sliced	100 g	4 oz	1 cup
OR Dried morels	50 g	2 oz	½ cup

Hint *Any type of wild mushrooms can be used. If serving a large number, then regular mushrooms can be mixed with the dried to reduce the cost. If using dried ones, they must be reconstituted by soaking them in hot water until they are soft.*

Crème fraîche or double cream	50 ml	2 fl oz	¼ cup

FOR THE VELOUTÉ			
Plain flour	15 g	½ oz	1 tbsp
Fish stock	350 ml	12 fl oz	1½ cups

Hint *If making this sauce to go with chicken, substitute chicken stock.*

Salt and freshly ground white pepper to taste			

TO FINISH			
Egg yolks	2	2	2
Crème fraîche or double cream	30 ml	2 tbsp	2 tbsp

To prepare the mushrooms Melt half the butter in a small saucepan. Add the onion and sauté until transparent. Add the morels and sauté for 1 minute. Stir in the *crème fraîche*. Set aside.

To prepare the velouté In a second saucepan, melt the remaining butter. Add the flour and cook without colouring for 1 minute. Add the fish stock and stir until the sauce thickens. Add salt and pepper to taste. Combine with the mushroom mixture. The sauce can be made in advance to this point. Just before serving, mix the egg yolks and *crème fraîche* and whisk gently into the warmed sauce. Correct the seasoning.

To serve Serve at once. Spoon the sauce onto each individual plate and lay the fish on top.

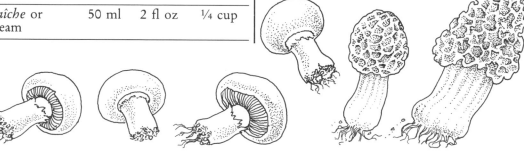

Les Sauces pour Volailles

SAUCES FOR CHICKEN

A chicken in the hands of a French chef is bound to result in a superb creation. It is not clear which came first the chicken or the sauce, but they live beautifully together. The sauces in this section bestow on the humble chicken flavours from fresh herbs, fruit, wine and whisky. The wide variation makes it possible to serve a dish to fit your mood.

The lighter style of cooking exemplified in these recipes should accompany fresh, light poultry. Buy a poussin, a spring chicken or a fresh young turkey, prepare one of the delightful sauces to complement it, and you have a meal fit for a gourmet. Chicken was once thought of as something one would never serve to guests. Happily, this type of thinking is becoming as old fashioned as the heavy sauces once used to disguise this tasty meat. I serve chicken often, especially when we are having a large meal with a hearty first course when a lighter course should follow. Many varied sauces are included. Try them and see how, in each case, the sauce enhances the mild, delicate flavour of the chicken.

Tarragon, morels, mustard and curry are traditionally used with chicken. These recipes, although using traditional ingredients, are more up-to-date in style. In other cases the use of fruit creates a sweet and sour effect that is fun and exotic.

By way of explanation

The shortened description in the *Sauce Supreme* recipe requires some additional explanation. A velouté is a basic sauce where a liquid is thickened. In this case, I have used chicken stock and have used as a thickening agent a roux blond. Flour is added to melted butter and is slowly cooked until it is a straw or café au lait colour. The stock is added slowly and, with additional cooking, a velouté consistency is reached.

Veloutés can also be made using vegetable or meat stock, wine or water as the liquid. The thickening agent can equally be a roux blanc (where the flour is not browned) or egg yolk. Note that if milk is used as the liquid together with a roux blanc, the sauce becomes a bechamel.

SAUCE SUPREME
Supreme Sauce

For poached, grilled, steamed or roast chicken

This well known French sauce is really a velouté made with cream added. It can be made in advance and gently warmed and served with the chicken. Because it is a delicately flavoured sauce, it is best served with a poached chicken. However, it can be served with a roast or grilled chicken.

Cooking time: 20 minutes: To serve 6

Opposite: *Filets de Porc à la Sauce aux Pêches et aux Abricots* (page 55).

Overleaf: *Poulet à la Sauce Chinoise* (page 56).

INGREDIENTS	METRIC	IMPERIAL	AMERICAN
Unsalted butter	25 g	1 oz	2 tbsp
Plain flour	25 g	1 oz	¼ cup
Chicken stock	350 ml	12 fl oz	1½ cups
Double cream	350 ml	12 fl oz	1½ cups
Juice from lemon	½	½	½
Nutmeg	¼ tsp	¼ tsp	¼ tsp
Pinch of cayenne			
Salt and freshly ground white pepper to taste			

Melt the butter in a saucepan. Add the flour and cook gently until the flour turns a straw or café au lait colour. Slowly pour in the chicken stock, mixing it in with a wire whisk. When it is well blended and thick, let cook for about 5 minutes to further cook the flour. Add the cream and simmer gently for 10 minutes. Add the remaining ingredients and taste for seasoning. Add more nutmeg, cayenne, salt or pepper as necessary.

To serve Serve the sauce warm poured over the chicken. If made in advance, gently warm, stirring constantly, and serve.

VOLAILLE POCHEE
Poached Chicken

Gently poaching a chicken keeps it beautifully moist. The liquid should never boil or the chicken will toughen. I use this method for chicken to be used in a salad. The chicken will not dry out even if prepared in advance.

Cooking time: 1 hour   To serve 6

INGREDIENTS	METRIC	IMPERIAL	AMERICAN
Chickens, each weighing about 1.1–1.4 kg/2½–3lb	2	2	2
Water to cover the chicken			
Dry white wine	125 ml	4 fl oz	½ cup
Carrots, sliced	2	2	2
Large onion, sliced	1	1	1
Sticks of celery, sliced	1	1	1
Whole peppercorns	6	6	6
Bay leaf	1	1	1
Parsley sprigs	2	2	2
Thyme sprigs	2	2	2

Place the chickens in a large pot big enough to hold both snugly. Add all the other ingredients. Bring the water to a boil and lower the heat. Simmer for 1 hour uncovered. Test the chickens to see if they are done. When pricked near the thigh joint the juices should run clear. Remove the chickens and carve.

Hint *If the chickens are to be served cold, allow them to cool down in the liquid. This can be done overnight in a cool place.*

To serve Serve hot with curry sauce or any of the other warm sauces for chicken.

Previous page: *Dinde à la Sauce Rose* (page 57).

Opposite: *Veau à la Sauce Hongroise* (page 62).

POULET A L'ESTRAGON
Tarragon Sauce with Chicken

For chicken or poussin

On one memorable trip to the South of France, we had the luck of finding a little restaurant run by a mother and her daughter. The food was bought fresh at the market each day and cooked with a wonderful light touch allowing all the natural flavours to dominate. I still remember the dish she made, *Poulet à l'Estragon*. The slightly anise flavour of fresh tarragon blends very well with chicken. This is a sauce that is created from the cooking juices of the chicken.

Cooking time: 50 minutes   To serve 6

INGREDIENTS	METRIC	IMPERIAL	AMERICAN
Light oil (corn or sunflower)	15 ml	1 tbsp	1 tbsp
Butter	25 g	1 oz	2 tbsp
Chickens, each weighing about 1.1–1.4 kg/2½–3 lb, quartered	2	2	2
Medium onion, sliced	1	1	1
Carrot, peeled and sliced	1	1	1
Dry white wine	175 ml	6 fl oz	¾ cup
Chicken stock	175 ml	6 fl oz	¾ cup
Fresh tarragon leaves, chopped	1 tbsp	1 tbsp	1 tbsp
Fresh chervil, if available (if using dried herbs, use half the amount)	1 tbsp	1 tbsp	1 tbsp
Salt and freshly ground white pepper to taste			

Heat the oil and butter in a sauté pan large enough to hold the chicken pieces. Brown the chicken pieces on both sides. Remove the chicken and add the onion and carrot. Sauté until they start to shrivel. Return the chicken to the pan and lower the heat, cover and let cook for 15–20 minutes or until the pieces are cooked through. Remove the white meat and leave the dark meat to cook a little longer. Test to make sure the chicken is done. When a knife is inserted into the flesh the juices will run clear. Remove the chicken and place on a warm serving platter. Cover with foil to keep warm. Pour off any fat remaining in the pan. Deglaze the pan with white wine. Scrape all the brown bits from the bottom of the pan. Add the chicken stock. Let the sauce boil hard for 3 minutes. Strain the sauce.

The recipe can be made ahead to this point. If you do this, then before serving, rewarm the chicken in the sauce.

Just before serving add the fresh herbs. Taste for seasoning. Add salt and pepper if necessary.

To serve Spoon the sauce over the chicken and serve.

SAUCE NORMANDE
Normandy Sauce with Roast Chicken

For roast chicken, guinea fowl or pheasant

The fruits of Normandy: apples, cider and cream, form the base of this sauce. It makes a perfect autumn dish.

Cooking time: 1¼ hours   To serve 4

INGREDIENTS	METRIC	IMPERIAL	AMERICAN
Peanut oil	30 ml	2 tbsp	2 tbsp
Salt and freshly ground black pepper to taste			
Roasting chicken	1.8 kg	4 lb	4 lb
Tart cooking apples (Bramleys if possible)	2	2	2
Shallots, chopped	5	5	5
Dry cider	425 ml	¾ pt	2 cups
Brown sugar	2 tsp	2 tsp	2 tsp
Cinnamon stick	1	1	1
Whole cloves	2	2	2
TO FINISH			
Potato flour or cornflour	1 tsp	1 tsp	1 tsp
Double cream	175 ml	6 fl oz	¾ cup

Heat the oil in a large heavy-bottomed casserole. Salt and pepper the inside of the chicken. Cut 3–4 slices from one of the apples and add to the cavity. Truss the chicken and brown it on all sides. Remove from the pot. Pour off any burned fat. Sauté the shallots until they start to shrivel. Do not brown them. Quarter and core the apples. Cut into eighths. Replace the chicken and add all the other ingredients except the po-tato flour and cream. Bring the liquid to the simmer and cover. Cook gently for 50 minutes. Check to see if the chicken is cooked. The juices should run clear when a knife is inserted into the thigh.

To finish Remove the chicken to a carving board, cover with foil and leave to rest. Sieve the sauce into a clean pan and taste. Skim as much fat as possible from the sauce. Mix the potato flour with a spoonful of the cream. Blend with the rest of the cream and add to the sauce over a gentle heat. Taste for seasoning. Add more salt and pepper if necessary.

To serve Carve the chicken and serve with the sauce spooned over the top.

POUSSIN AU VINAIGRE DE VIN DE XERES

*Sherry Wine Vinegar Sauce
with Poussin*

For young poussin or baby chickens

Sherry wine vinegar has become popular with the new emphasis on light sauces. It blends well with the cooking juices of the baby chickens and fresh herbs to create a fragrant sauce.

Cooking time: 50 minutes   To serve 6

INGREDIENTS	METRIC	IMPERIAL	AMERICAN
Oil	15 ml	1 tbsp	1 tbsp
Unsalted butter	25 g	1 oz	2 tbsp
Salt and freshly ground black pepper to taste			
Small poussin	6	6	6
Cloves garlic, whole	8	8	8
Large onion, thinly sliced	1	1	1
Bay leaf	1	1	1
Sprigs of fresh thyme (if using dried, use only 1 sprig or 1 tsp)	2	2	2
Sherry wine vinegar	60 ml	4 tbsp	4 tbsp
Chicken stock	225 ml	8 fl oz	1 cup
TO FINISH			
Castor sugar	2 tsp	2 tsp	2 tsp
Sherry wine vinegar	30 ml	2 tbsp	2 tbsp
TO GARNISH			
Fresh parsley and thyme, chopped	2 tbsp	2 tbsp	2 tbsp

Heat the oil and butter in a large sauté pan. Salt and pepper the inside of the poussin and add 1 whole garlic clove to each cavity. Truss the poussin. Brown each poussin one at a time in the pan.

Hint *If you do not have a pan large enough for 6 poussin, then divide the oil and butter in half and use two pans.*

Remove the poussin when they are golden and add the onion. Sauté the onion until it is transparent. Return the poussin to the pan and add the bay leaf, thyme, wine vinegar, chicken stock and remaining garlic. Cover and simmer slowly for 30 minutes or until the poussin are cooked. Test by sticking a knife into one of the thighs. If the juices run clear, it is cooked. When the poussin are finished, remove them from the pan to a warmed serving platter. Untie them and remove the garlic. Cover the poussin with foil to keep warm.

To finish Dissolve the sugar in the remaining vinegar. Make sure it is completely dissolved. Set aside. Skim as much fat as possible from the juices and bring the liquid to the boil in the pan. Reduce the sauce by one third. Remove the bay leaf and thyme. Pour the sauce with the onions and garlic into a liquidiser and add the sweetened vinegar. Blend for several seconds until the sauce thickens. Strain. Return to a clean saucepan to heat through. Taste for seasoning. Add salt and pepper as necessary.

To serve Spoon the sauce around the poussin and sprinkle with freshly chopped parsley and thyme.

SAUCE AU WHISKY
Whisky Sauce

For poached, steamed, sautéed or grilled chicken

The addition of a little whisky lends an interesting flavour to a cream sauce.

Cooking time: 15 minutes   To serve 6

INGREDIENTS	METRIC	IMPERIAL	AMERICAN
Unsalted butter	50 g	2 oz	¼ cup
Mushrooms, washed and sliced	225 g	8 oz	2 cups
Plain flour	20 g	¾ oz	1½ tbsp
Good chicken stock	275 ml	½ pt	1¼ cups
Double cream	175 ml	6 fl oz	¾ cup
Whisky	60 ml	4 tbsp	4 tbsp
Salt and freshly ground white pepper to taste			

Melt half the butter in a frying pan. Add the mushrooms and sauté for 2 minutes. Stir them gently with a fork being careful not to break them up. Remove from the heat and set aside. Melt the remaining butter and add the flour. Cook for 1 minute. Slowly pour in the chicken stock, whisking constantly. When thoroughly mixed and thickened, cook for another minute to cook the flour. Add the cream and whisk. Add the whisky, salt and pepper. Simmer gently for 5 minutes. Add the mushrooms and taste for seasoning. Add more salt and pepper if necessary.

To serve Serve the sauce warm, poured over the chicken. If using roast or grilled chicken, then pour some of the sauce on individual plates and place the chicken on the sauce. This will preserve the crisp skin.

POULET DIJONNAISE
Dijon Chicken

Strong, flavourful dijon mustard gives this sauce a characteristic flavour. However, if you feel like experimenting, then try some of the different kinds of mustards on the market.

Cooking time: 30 minutes   To serve 4

INGREDIENTS	METRIC	IMPERIAL	AMERICAN
Butter	25 g	1 oz	2 tbsp
Chicken, quartered	1.4 kg	3 lb	3 lb
Dijon mustard	15 ml	1 tbsp	1 tbsp
Coarse-grain mustard (moutarde de meaux)	15 ml	1 tbsp	1 tbsp
Vermouth	75 ml	3 fl oz	6 tbsp
Crème fraiche (or double cream)	120 ml	4 fl oz	½ cup
Salt and freshly ground black pepper to taste			

Melt the butter in a heavy-bottomed casserole. Brown the chicken pieces on all sides. Pour off any excess fat. Add the mustard and vermouth and bring the liquid to a simmer. Cover and simmer for 15 minutes. Remove the white meat and cook the dark meat for another 5 minutes. Test the meat to see that it is done. Stick a knife in the top of the thigh near the joint. If the juices run clear, the chicken is cooked. Remove the meat to a serving platter and cover to keep warm. Skim as much fat as possible from the cooking juices. Add the *crème fraiche*, salt and pepper to taste. Mix well. Taste the sauce for seasoning. If you like a stronger mustard flavour, then add more mustard at this point.

To serve Strain the sauce. Spoon some sauce onto a serving platter and place the chicken on top. Serve the rest in a sauce boat.

SAUCE AU CURRY
Curry Sauce

For poached chicken, fish or vegetables

The cooking revolution in France during the last 10 years brought many exotic flavours to French tables. Many of the top restaurants started serving dishes with a hint of curry which was very pleasing using this spice sparingly brings out subtle nuances of flavour. This sauce can be made in advance and used for many different dishes.

Cooking time: 25 minutes   To serve 6

INGREDIENTS	METRIC	IMPERIAL	AMERICAN
Unsalted butter	50 g	2 oz	¼ cup
Shallots, chopped	3	3	3
Curry powder	1 tbsp	1 tbsp	1 tbsp
Plain flour	1 tbsp	1 tbsp	1 tbsp
Chicken stock	350 ml	12 fl oz	1½ cups
Large tart cooking apple (Bramley), peeled and cut into 1.2 cm/½ in cubes	1	1	1
Crème fraîche (or double cream)	90 ml	6 tbsp	6 tbsp
Salt and freshly ground black pepper to taste			
Juice from lemon	½	½	½

Melt half the butter in a saucepan. Add the shallots and sauté until they start to shrivel. Add the curry powder. Cook for 2–3 minutes. Stir in the flour. Cook for 1 minute. Slowly pour in the stock, stirring constantly. Let the sauce simmer gently for 20 minutes, stirring occasionally.

Melt the rest of the butter in a small pan and sauté the apple cubes. Try not to let them break up. Turn them gently with a fork. Add them to the sauce. Add the cream, salt and pepper to taste. Add half the lemon juice. Taste. If a sharper flavour is desired, then add more lemon juice and correct the seasoning.

To serve Serve in a sauce boat with poached chicken (recipe page 49) or whatever food you have chosen.

SAUCE A LA COMPOTE DE POMMES
Apple Sauce with Lemon Juice

For grilled chicken, turkey or pork

Caramelised apples and leeks give this savoury sauce a hint of sweetness. It provides an interesting accent to grilled meats.

Cooking time: 30 minutes   To serve 6

INGREDIENTS	METRIC	IMPERIAL	AMERICAN
Tart cooking apples (Bramleys are best)	4	4	4
Lemons	2	2	2
Unsalted butter	50 g	2 oz	¼ cup
Leeks, washed and sliced	225 g	8 oz	2 cups
Castor sugar	2 tsp	2 tsp	2 tsp
Chicken stock	175 ml	6 fl oz	¾ cup
Powdered cinnamon	1 tsp	1 tsp	1 tsp
Salt and freshly ground black pepper to taste			
Crème fraîche	90 ml	6 tbsp	6 tbsp

Peel, quarter and core the apples. Peel 2–3 thin strips of rind from the lemons leaving the white pith behind. Squeeze the lemons. Place the lemon juice and lemon strips with half the apples in a saucepan. Cover and simmer gently for 15–20 minutes or until a sauce is formed. Do not evaporate the juices. Meanwhile heat half the butter in a pan and sauté the leeks until they soften. Add half the sugar and continue to sauté until they are golden and syrupy. Remove the lemon rind from the apples. Combine the chicken stock, cooked apples and leeks in a food processor or liquidiser. Season with cinnamon, salt and pepper. Return to a low heat and add the *crème fraiche*. Cut the remaining apples into cubes. Melt the remaining butter in a pan. Sprinkle the apples with the remaining sugar and gently sauté. Add the caramelised apples to the sauce and taste for seasoning. Add more as necessary.

To serve This sauce can be made several days in advance and gently warmed when needed.

Sauce aux Peches et aux Abricots
— *Peach and Apricot Sauce* —

For poultry, pheasant, duck or pork

Sweet fruit sauces make a delightful change to the usual sauces served with poultry. The sauce can be made in advance and warmed and served when needed. Fresh peaches and apricots would be best for this sauce, but since these have such a short season, I have used dried fruit in the recipe which gives an excellent result.

Cooking time: 1¼ hours   To serve 6

INGREDIENTS	METRIC	IMPERIAL	AMERICAN
Dried apricots	100 g	4 oz	1 cup
Dried peaches	100 g	4 oz	1 cup
Water to cover the fruit			
White wine vinegar	50 ml	2 fl oz	¼ cup
Castor sugar	100 g	4 oz	½ cup
Dry sherry	50 ml	2 fl oz	¼ cup
Stem ginger in syrup, chopped	1 tbsp	1 tbsp	1 tbsp
TO GARNISH			
1 jar spiced peaches or apricots	425 g	14½ oz	14 ½ oz

Place the apricots and peaches in a saucepan and cover with water. Bring the water to the boil and simmer for about ½ hour or until the fruit is reconstituted.

Hint *Buy the best quality dried fruit possible. The fruit should be full and flavourful after it has simmered.*

Drain the fruit, reserving the water. Place the fruit back in the pan and add the wine vinegar and sugar. Bring the mixture to a simmer. Cover and simmer gently, stirring occasionally, for 30 minutes. Add the sherry and ginger and simmer for 10 minutes. Purée in a food processor or blender or pass through a food mill. If the sauce is too thick, then thin it with some of the reserved water.

To serve Carve the chicken or whatever you have chosen to serve, and spoon the sauce over it. Decorate the serving platter with the spiced fruit.

SAUCE CHINOISE

Savoury Pineapple Sauce

For chicken, duck or pork

With the advent of nouvelle cuisine, chefs sought near and far for new taste sensations. The inspiration for this sauce is Chinese with a definite French flavour.

Cooking time: 30 minutes   To serve 6

INGREDIENTS	METRIC	IMPERIAL	AMERICAN
Ripe fresh pineapple, medium sized, with the flesh cut into cubes	1	1	1
Chicken stock	225 ml	8 fl oz	1 cup
Light brown sugar	75 g	3 oz	$1/3$ cup
White wine vinegar	30 ml	2 tbsp	2 tbsp
Good quality soy sauce	10 ml	2 tsp	2 tsp
TO FINISH			
Potato flour or cornflour	2 tsp	2 tsp	2 tsp
Chicken stock	30 ml	2 tbsp	2 tbsp
Sweet red pepper cut into julienne strips	1	1	1

Divide the pineapple cubes in half, saving one half for decoration. Place the other half in a saucepan with the chicken stock and brown sugar. Bring to a boil and reduce to a simmer. Simmer gently for 15–20 minutes or until the pineapple is soft. Add the wine vinegar and soy sauce. Strain into a clean pan. Simmer for 5 minutes.

To finish Mix the potato flour with the stock and pour into the sauce. Bring the sauce to the simmer and cook until thick. The sauce can be made ahead to this point and reheated. Add the pepper and reserved pineapple to warm in the sauce just before serving.

To serve Spoon the warm sauce over the poultry, or whatever you have chosen to serve.

DINDE A LA SAUCE ROSE
Turkey with Vermouth and Cranberries

For turkey or duck

Cranberries are a traditional accompaniment to turkey. This sauce, however, has only a slight hint of cranberries. It is a light clear sauce that goes well with the turkey meat.

To serve 8–10

INGREDIENTS	METRIC	IMPERIAL	AMERICAN
Turkey	4.5–5.4 kg	10–12 lb	10–12 lb
Butter	75–100 g	3–4 oz	1/3–1/2 cup
Salt and freshly ground black pepper to taste			
Large onion, sliced	1	1	1
Large carrots, sliced	2	2	2
Chicken stock	575 ml	1 pt	2½ cups
Dry vermouth	350 ml	12 fl oz	1½ cups
Fresh cranberries	225 g	8 oz	2 cups
Castor sugar	25 g	2 tbsp	2 tbsp
Potato flour or cornflour	2 tsp	2 tsp	2 tsp
Chicken stock	30 ml	2 tbsp	2 tbsp

Heat the oven to 180°C/350°F/gas mark 4. Rub the butter all over the turkey. Clean any pin feathers from the turkey. Wipe inside and out. Salt and pepper the cavity and truss the bird. Place the onion and carrots on the bottom of a roasting tin. Place the turkey on a rack in the tin. Pour about 275 ml/10 fl oz/1¼ cups of stock into the tin. Place in the oven and roast for about 20 minutes per 450 g/1 lb, basting the turkey every 20 minutes. Add more stock if the roasting tin looks dry. Test the turkey by sticking a knife into the thigh. It is done when the juices run clear. Take it out and let it rest while the sauce is made. Place foil over it to keep it warm.

To make the sauce Place the roasting tin on a hob and pour in the vermouth. Deglaze the pan scraping up all the brown bits from the bottom. Add the cranberries and sugar and reduce the sauce by half. Add the remaining stock and reduce by half again. Add salt and pepper to taste. If the sauce tastes weak or watery, reduce further. Strain into a clean pan. Mix the potato flour with the 30 ml/2 tbsp of cold chicken stock. Pour into the pan and bring to a simmer, stirring constantly. The sauce will thicken. Correct the seasoning.

To serve Carve the turkey and serve with the warmed sauce.

Les Sauces pour les Viandes

SAUCES FOR MEAT

The heartier meats remind me of a cold winter's night with a fire in the fireplace and hungry guests sitting enjoying a lovely meal. This is the perfect setting for a superb treat for you and your guests. Isn't this the scene for a beautiful steak grilled to perfection, crisp and brown on the outside and rare inside with a mushroom and port sauce? This sauce will match the steak's robust flavour without masking it, and can be made in five minutes. All you need is a glass of fine red wine to round off your dinner and create a perfect evening.

To partake of this elegance does not mean hours in the kitchen. Whenever I'm in a hurry and want to prepare an elegant dish quickly, I plan to simply grill or roast a good piece of meat and serve it with a delicious sauce that has been previously prepared and is waiting in the refrigerator or freezer.

With this in mind, I have included many sauces that can either be made partially or totally in advance and refrigerated or frozen, as well as sauces that can be made in minutes. In this section I have combined the presentation of sauces for veal, beef, pork and lamb, because many of them are interchangeable. Try a piquant Creole Sauce to go with lamb or an Onion Sauce for beef. If you find yourself with no sauce in the refrigerator or freezer, whip up a Bernaise Sauce in minutes in the food processor.

For those times when you have a few more minutes, there are the more traditional recipes such as Romaine, Chasseur, Diable and Zingara Sauces. Their rich flavour is a treat that is worth the preparation time.

All the sauces in this section will complement the meats you choose and help you to serve a lovely meal with ease.

VEAU AU CALVADOS
—— Veal with Calvados Sauce ——

For veal or chicken

Normandy is famous for its apples. One of the by-products is Calvados, an apple brandy, very popular in that area. This dish is very quick and easy, and produces a lovely light main course. The sauce is created from the juices left from sautéing veal escalopes.

Cooking time: 5–10 minutes   To serve 6

INGREDIENTS	METRIC	IMPERIAL	AMERICAN
Veal escalopes, each about 175 g/6 oz	6	6	6
Unsalted butter	50 g	2 oz	¼ cup
Salt and freshly ground black pepper to taste			
Calvados (or other apple brandy)	75 ml	3 fl oz	6 tbsp
Crème fraîche (or double cream)	75 ml	3 fl oz	6 tbsp

58

Take a meat bat or heavy saucepan and with a sliding motion flatten the escalopes.

Hint *Slide the meat bat away from you as it touches the meat. If you use an up and down motion, the meat is likely to tear.*

Heat the butter in a heavy-bottomed frying pan. When it is sizzling, add one escalope. Move it around the pan so that it doesn't stick to the bottom. Cook for 1 minute and turn. Move again to prevent sticking.

Hint *Moving the meat as soon as it touches the bottom of the pan prevents bits sticking to the pan and burning. This will prevent the resulting sauce from having a burned or bitter flavour.*

Cook the second side for 1 minute and remove to a serving platter. Cover with foil to keep warm. Continue to cook all of the escalopes in this manner. Salt and pepper the cooked meat.

To make the sauce Place the escalopes in the pan, pour in the Calvados and flambé.

Hint *To flambé, tip the pan so that the warmed Calvados catches the flame. Turn off the heat and let the flames die down. If using an electric hob, throw a lighted match into the warmed Calvados, remembering to remove the match after the flames have died.*

Place the veal on the serving platter and cover. Reduce the Calvados to about 15 ml/1 tbsp. Add the *crème fraîche* to the pan and deglaze. Scrape all the browned bits from the bottom of the pan. Taste for the seasoning and add salt and pepper as necessary.

Hint *This dish should take about 5 minutes to make. Try not to overcook the veal. It is best made and served immediately.*

To serve Pour the sauce over the veal and serve immediately.

SAUCE ZINGARA
Zingara Sauce

For veal, beef or chicken

The name 'zingara' has always intrigued me. Since it means a gypsy, one can only surmise that the idea for this sauce came to us from this nomadic people. Mushrooms, smoked ham, pickled tongue and tomato purée transform the brown sauce by providing colour and zip. It goes very well with grilled meat.

Cooking time: 10 minutes   To serve 6

INGREDIENTS	METRIC	IMPERIAL	AMERICAN
Brown sauce (page 16)	275 ml	½ pt	1¼ cups
Tomato purée	150 ml	¼ pt	⅔ cup
Madeira or dry sherry	30 ml	2 tbsp	2 tbsp
Mushrooms, cut in julienne strips	25 g	1 oz	2 tbsp
Cooked ham, cut in julienne strips	25 g	1 oz	2 tbsp
Pickled tongue, cut in julienne strips	25 g	2 oz	2 tbsp
Salt and freshly ground black pepper to taste			
TO GARNISH			
Sprinkling of paprika			

Warm the brown sauce in a pan and add the tomato purée and madeira. Add the julienne mushrooms and meat. Simmer for 2–3 minutes. Taste for seasoning and add salt and pepper as needed. If making this in advance, rewarm it gently without boiling so that the julienne meat and mushrooms do not break up.

To serve Spoon over cooked meat and sprinkle with paprika to garnish.

COTES DE VEAU AU MADERE

Veal Chops with Madeira and Orange Marmalade

For veal, beef or pork

This is a wonderful last minute dish as the sauce whisks up in minutes. It can, though, be prepared a couple of hours in advance and gently rewarmed.

Cooking time: 20 minutes   To serve 6

INGREDIENTS	METRIC	IMPERIAL	AMERICAN
Unsalted butter	50 g	2 oz	¼ cup
Light vegetable oil	25 ml	1 fl oz	2 tbsp
Veal chops	6	6	6
Salt and freshly ground black pepper to taste			
Small onion, finely chopped	1	1	1
Madeira wine	175 ml	6 fl oz	¾ cup
Chicken stock	175 ml	6 fl oz	¾ cup
Orange marmalade	40 g	3 tbsp	3 tbsp
Crème fraîche (or double cream	75 ml	3 fl oz	6 tbsp
TO GARNISH			
6 thin slices of orange cut from 1 orange			

Heat the butter and oil in a frying pan. Add one chop and move it as it touches the pan. This will prevent the meat from sticking and burning on the bottom of the pan. Cook on a high heat for 1 minute. Turn and move it again. Cook for 1 minute. Salt and pepper the cooked side. Add another chop to the pan and continue cooking the same way until all chops are browned. Lower the heat and cook the chops until they are just slightly pink inside and still juicy, about 5 minutes. Remove the chops to a heated serving platter and cover with foil to keep warm.

To make the sauce Add the onion to the frying pan and cook until transparent. Add the madeira, stock and marmalade to the onion. Scrape up the brown bits that are in the pan. Raise the heat and reduce the liquid by one third. The recipe can be made in advance to this point. When ready to serve, add the *crème fraîche*, salt and pepper. Taste for seasoning and add more if necessary. Warm the orange slices in the sauce for 1 minute.

Hint *If preparing the dish in advance, slightly undercook the chops and make the sauce. Before serving, warm the chops in the sauce until fully cooked and then serve. It is best to make this dish no more than 2 hours in advance. Do not refrigerate the meat while it is waiting.*

To serve Spoon the warm sauce over the chops and decorate with orange slices.

ESCALOPES DE VEAU AUX POMMES

Veal Escalopes with White Wine and Apples

For veal escalopes, grilled chicken or pork fillets

A simple sauce made from the juices of the cooked meat plus white wine and apples lends a delicate touch to veal escalopes. Because it takes no more than 20 minutes to make this dish, I suggest it be made at the last minute. It can, though, be made ahead and gently warmed. Try not to overcook the veal. It should be juicy and pink with a slight crustiness to the surface.

Cooking time: 20 minutes   To serve 6

INGREDIENTS	METRIC	IMPERIAL	AMERICAN
Veal escalopes, each about 176 g/6 oz	6	6	6
Unsalted butter	50 g	2 oz	¼ cup
Shallots, finely chopped	3	3	3
Tart apples, peeled and sliced	2	2	2
Dry white wine	125 ml	4 fl oz	½ cup
Crème fraîche	75 ml	3 fl oz	6 tbsp
Salt and freshly ground white pepper to taste			

Ask your butcher to bat out the veal escalopes or do this yourself. Take a meat bat and with a sliding motion flatten the escalopes.

Hint *Slide the meat bat away from you as it touches the meat. If you use an up and down motion, the meat is likely to tear. A heavy saucepan can be used instead of a meat bat.*

Heat the butter in a heavy-bottomed frying pan. When it is sizzling add one escalope. Move it around the pan so that it doesn't stick to the bottom. Cook for 1 minute and turn. Move again to prevent sticking.

Hint *Moving the meat as soon as it touches the bottom of the pan prevents bits sticking to the pan and burning. This will prevent the resulting sauce from having a burned or bitter flavour.*

Cook the second side for 1 minute and remove to a serving platter. Cover with foil to keep warm, while you cook the remaining escalopes.

To make the sauce Sauté the shallots in the frying pan until they are transparent, adding more butter if necessary. Add the apple slices and gently turn them in the butter. Use a fork to gently turn the apples. This will help to stop them breaking up. Add the white wine and reduce by about one half. Add the *crème fraîche*. Add salt and pepper to taste. The recipe can be made ahead to this point. When ready to serve, slip the escalopes into the sauce and warm them through.

To serve Serve at once. Return the meat to the serving platter and spoon the sauce over the escalopes.

61

SAUCE HONGROISE
Hungarian Paprika Sauce
For all types of veal or chicken

Good Hungarian paprika is quite different from the bland type one usually sees. Its aromatic flavour adds the essential touch to this sauce. It is well worth going to a speciality shop and getting some. Ask for imported Hungarian paprika, either the hot or the mild type according to your taste. This sauce can be made in advance and frozen or kept for a day. It improves if made in advance. Gently warm it when needed.

Cooking time: 35 minutes   To serve 6

INGREDIENTS	METRIC	IMPERIAL	AMERICAN
Unsalted butter	50 g	2 oz	¼ cup
Medium onion, chopped	1	1	1
Plain flour	25 g	1 oz	¼ cup
Hungarian paprika	1 tbsp	1 tbsp	1 tbsp
Good chicken stock	850 ml	1½ pt	3¾ cups
Bouquet garni (made with 1 bay leaf, sprig fresh thyme, several parsley stalks)			
Dry white wine	75 ml	3 fl oz	6 tbsp
Crème fraîche	75 ml	3 fl oz	6 tbsp
Salt and freshly ground black pepper to taste			

Melt the butter in a heavy-bottomed saucepan and add the onion. Sauté until the onion is transparent. Add the flour and paprika and cook for several minutes to cook the flour and release the flavour of the paprika.

Hint *When using powdered spices such as paprika or curry powder, they should be heated. This can be done either in the saucepan as above, or on a plate in a low oven for a few minutes, if the powder is to be added to the sauce at a later stage. This allows all the flavour to develop.*

Add the chicken stock little by little, stirring constantly. Add the bouquet garni and let the sauce bubble gently for 20 minutes, skimming any impurities that rise to the top. Add the white wine and reduce the sauce by about half. This will take about 10 minutes. Strain. The sauce can be made ahead to this point and kept a day or frozen. It may thicken on standing. Add a little more chicken stock to thin.

To finish Add the *crème fraîche* and salt and pepper. Taste for seasoning and add more if necessary.

To serve Serve the warm sauce over cooked veal or chicken.

SAUCE BEARNAISE
Bearnaise Sauce
For grilled beef, chicken, fish or egg dishes

This is a modern version of the celebrated *Sauce Béarnaise*. Basically a bearnaise is a hollandaise sauce made with different herbs and the addition of white wine. By substituting wine vinegar and vermouth an intriguing flavour results.

Cooking time: 25 minutes   To serve 6

INGREDIENTS	METRIC	IMPERIAL	AMERICAN
Sherry wine vinegar (raspberry wine vinegar, white wine vinegar or any type you choose)	60 ml	4 tbsp	4 tbsp
Dry vermouth	90 ml	6 tbsp	6 tbsp
Shallots, finely chopped	2	2	2
Fresh tarragon, chopped	1 tsp	1 tsp	1 tsp
OR Dried tarragon	½ tsp	½ tsp	½ tsp
Fresh chervil (if available)	1 tsp	1 tsp	1 tsp
Egg yolks	3	3	3
Salt and freshly ground white pepper to taste			
Unsalted butter, at room temperature and cut into cubes	175g	6 oz	¼ cup

Hint *As with hollandaise sauce, there are a few points to remember. The egg yolks must be warmed very gently. If the heat is too high they will curdle. The second point is to remember that the yolks can only absorb the butter slowly. If too much butter is added at one time, the sauce will not thicken.*

Place the vinegar, vermouth, shallots, tarragon and chervil in a small enamel or stainless steel saucepan. Bring to the boil and reduce to about 30 ml/2 tbsp. Strain and set aside to cool. Place the egg yolks in a saucepan and place in a bain marie over a low heat. Whisk to warm the eggs. Add the reduced vinegar and wine and a pinch of salt. Whisking constantly, add a cube of butter. As this is absorbed add another cube of butter. Continue slowly in this way until all the butter is absorbed.

Hint *It is a good idea to test the water of the bain marie with your finger. If the water is hot to the touch, then take the pan out and wait for the water to cool.*

Once the sauce has thickened, take off the heat and continue to whisk until it has cooled. Taste for seasoning and add salt and pepper as necessary. If a sharper flavour is desired, add more vinegar.

The sauce can be made 1–2 hours ahead of time and kept warm in a bain marie filled with warm water. When needed, simply raise the heat and whisk constantly until the sauce is warmed through. If you have a problem with the sauce, turn to the section on Hints for Hollandaise on page 37.

Hint *The sauce can be made in a food processor. See the instructions for Food Processor Bearnaise, page 64.*

To serve Pour into a sauce boat and serve warm with the meat.

SAUCE CHORON
Choron Sauce

This is a Bearnaise Sauce that has had 30 ml/ 2 tbsp of tomato purée added at the end.

SAUCE PALOISE
Paloise Sauce

For lamb and beef

This is a Bearnaise Sauce that uses mint in place of the tarragon.

SAUCE BEARNAISE 2
Food Processor
Bearnaise Sauce

For grilled beef, chicken, fish or egg dishes

The worry of making a Bearnaise Sauce at the last minute is alleviated with this quick, foolproof method. Have all the ingredients measured and ready then make the sauce a few minutes before it is needed.

Cooking time: 5 minutes   To serve 6

INGREDIENTS	METRIC	IMPERIAL	AMERICAN
Sherry wine vinegar (or a fruit wine vinegar)	60 ml	4 tbsp	4 tbsp
Dry vermouth	90 ml	6 tbsp	6 tbsp
Shallots, finely chopped	2	2	2
Fresh tarragon, chopped	1 tsp	1 tsp	1 tsp
OR Dried tarragon	½ tsp	½ tsp	½ tsp
Fresh chervil (if available)	1 tsp	1 tsp	1 tsp
Egg yolks	3	3	3
Unsalted butter	175 g	6 oz	¾ cup
Salt and freshly ground white pepper to taste			

Place the vinegar, vermouth, shallots, tarragon and chervil in a small enamel or stainless steel saucepan. Bring to the boil and reduce to about 30 ml/2 tbsp. Strain into the food processor. This can be done in advance. Cool slightly. Add the egg yolks. Process the yolks until they are thick and creamy, about 1–2 minutes. Heat the butter to sizzling. With the machine running, slowly pour the butter through the feed tube, stopping every few seconds to let the machine incorporate the ingredients. When all the butter is poured in, add salt and pepper to taste and serve immediately.

Hint *The butter must be hot enough to cook the egg yolks slightly. However, it must be poured slowly and carefully into the food processor to prevent the heat curdling the eggs. Watch the eggs as the machine runs and you will know when to pour and when to slow down. The entire process takes about 2–3 minutes.*

Opposite: *Boeuf à le Sauce aux Champignons et au Porto* (page 69).

Overleaf: *Rond de Gigot au Porto* (page 75).

COTES DE VEAU AU ROQUEFORT
Veal with Roquefort Sauce

For veal, steak or pork

Many restaurants serve this dish with the cheese slightly melted on top of the meat. I find that the cheese overpowers the flavour of the meat when it is served this way. In this recipe the cheese is melted in as part of the sauce and a more subtle flavour is developed. Any type of blue-veined cheese can be substituted for Roquefort.

Cooking time: 30 minutes   To serve 6

INGREDIENTS	METRIC	IMPERIAL	AMERICAN
Oil	15 ml	1 tbsp	1 tbsp
Unsalted butter	15 g	½ oz	1 tbsp
Veal chops, each weighing about 150–175 g/5–6 oz	6	6	6
Salt and freshly ground black pepper to taste			
Shallots, finely chopped	2	2	2
Medium cider	75 ml	3 fl oz	6 tbsp
Brown stock	75 ml	3 fl oz	6 tbsp

Hint *Use chicken stock if you do not have a good brown stock available. Beef stock cubes tend to be salty and with the cheese the dish will become very salty.*

Crème fraîche or double cream	45 ml	3 tbsp	3 tbsp
Roquefort cheese, cut into cubes	50 g	2 oz	½ cup

Heat the oil and butter in a large frying pan. When the fat is sizzling, add one veal chop. Move it in the pan to prevent sticking. Let cook for 2 minutes. Turn the chop and move it again. Add the next chop.

Hint *Each time fresh meat is added, move it with two spoons so that it does not stick to the pan. Any pieces that do stick will burn and spoil your sauce.*

Salt and pepper the cooked side of the meat. Continue to brown all the veal in this way. Each piece should cook for 5–7 minutes in all. Remove the veal to a warm serving platter and cover with foil to keep warm.

To make the sauce Pour off any extra fat and add the shallots. Sauté until they are transparent. Deglaze the pan with the cider, scraping up all the brown bits on the bottom. Add the stock and reduce the liquid by half. Add the *crème fraiche* and cheese. Simmer to melt the cheese completely. Season with pepper.

To serve Spoon the sauce over the veal and serve immediately.

Previous page: *Broccoli à la Sauce Moutarde* (page 79). *Haricots Verts à la Sauce à la Poitrine Fumé* (page 80). *Pommes de Terre au Beurre à l'Estragon* (page 82).

Opposite: *Artichauts à la Sauce au Citron* (page 80).

SAUCE CREOLE
Creole Sauce

For veal, chicken, lamb or beef

This sauce has a rich tomato base with a blend of onions, peppers and celery. It is very good made a day ahead which allows time for all the flavours to develop.

Cooking time: 45 minutes   To serve 6

INGREDIENTS	METRIC	IMPERIAL	AMERICAN
Unsalted butter	25 g	1 oz	2 tbsp
Olive oil	15 ml	1 tbsp	1 tbsp
Medium onion, finely chopped	1	1	1
Clove garlic, crushed	1	1	1
Sticks of celery, finely diced	2	2	2
Small green pepper, seeded and finely diced	1	1	1
Small red peppers, seeded and finely diced	2	2	2
Fresh tomatoes	5–6	5–6	5–6
OR Tinned tomatoes	400 g	14 oz	14 oz
Bay leaf	1	1	1
Dry sherry	15 ml	1 tbsp	1 tbsp
Tomato purée (optional)	5 ml	1 tsp	1 tsp
Small tin pimentoes, finely diced	200 g	7 oz	7 oz
Salt and freshly ground black pepper to taste			

Heat the butter and olive oil in a heavy-bottomed saucepan and sauté the onion until transparent. This will take about 10 minutes. Add the garlic and cook for a few more minutes.

Add the celery and peppers, and sauté for 2–3 minutes. Skin and quarter the tomatoes and add to the sauce with the bay leaf and sherry.

Hint *Skin the tomatoes by placing them one at a time into boiling water. Leave for 10–12 seconds, then lift out and plunge into ice water and peel.*

Simmer the sauce gently, covered, for 10 minutes. Remove the lid and continue to cook for 10–15 minutes or until the sauce thickens. If the sauce is too thin, simply let it simmer for a few more minutes without a lid until it thickens. If using tinned or winter tomatoes, you may want to add the tomato purée for a richer colour and flavour.

To finish Add the pimentoes, salt and pepper and cook for another minute. Taste for seasoning, adding more salt and pepper if necessary.

To serve Serve warm over veal, chicken, lamb or beef.

SAUCE AUX ECHALOTES
Shallot Sauce

For sautéed or grilled beef

One of my husband's favourite recipes is *Onglet aux Echalotes*. *Onglet* is a cut of beef that is difficult to find because most butchers take it home for themselves. It is tougher than rump steak or fillet steak, but has much more flavour. In England it is called rump skirt and is well worth trying. The shallot sauce forms a perfect accompaniment for beef.

Cooking time: 15 minutes   To serve 6

INGREDIENTS	METRIC	IMPERIAL	AMERICAN
Unsalted butter	50 g	2 oz	¼ cup
Rump skirt (entrêcote, rump steak, fillet steak or any type of grilling steak)	1.1 kg	2½ lb	2½ lb
Salt and freshly ground black pepper to taste			
Shallots, finely chopped	75 g	3 oz	⅓ cup
Red wine vinegar	45 ml	3 tbsp	3 tbsp
Red wine	225 ml	8 fl oz	1 cup
Beef stock	225 ml	8 fl oz	1 cup

Heat the butter in a heavy-bottomed frying pan. When it is sizzling, add the steak. Move it as soon as it touches the pan to prevent it sticking. Brown for 2 minutes and turn. Move the steak again and let brown for another 2 minutes. Salt and pepper the cooked side. Lower the heat and cook until done.

Hint *The length of cooking time depends on the size of the steak and personal preference.*

In this recipe the rump skirt will take about 15 minutes for rare and longer for those who like it more well done.

Remove the steak to a warm platter, cover with foil, and let rest before carving.

To make the sauce Pour off any excess fat and sauté the shallots in the frying pan. Cook them until they are transparent. Deglaze the pan with the wine vinegar, scraping up any brown bits that are left on the bottom. Add the wine and reduce by half. Add the stock and reduce again. Season with salt and pepper. Taste for seasoning and add more if necessary.

To serve Carve the steak and spoon the sauce over it.

Hint *If you prefer, the steak can be grilled indoors or on a barbecue and the sauce made separately. Pour the juices from the carved meat into the sauce. The sauce can be made in advance in this case.*

SAUCE A L'OIGNON
Onion Sauce

For beef or other roast or grilled meat

The aroma of steak grilling on the barbecue is always welcome. I often feel a tangy sauce is nice to serve with the charcoal flavour. To make your entertaining even more fun, the sauce can be made a day in advance and rewarmed. This is a robust sauce that will also go with any type of roast or grilled meat.

Cooking time: 45 minutes   To serve 6

INGREDIENTS	METRIC	IMPERIAL	AMERICAN
Smoked streaky bacon	225 g	8 oz	8 oz
Large onions, thinly sliced	2	2	2
Plain flour	1 tbsp	1 tbsp	1 tbsp
Tomato purée	15 ml	1 tbsp	1 tbsp
Dry red wine	50 ml	2 fl oz	¼ cup
Brown stock	425 ml	¾ pt	1¾ cups
Red wine vinegar	10 ml	2 tsp	2 tsp
Salt and freshly ground black pepper to taste			

Cut the rind off the bacon and slice into 2 cm/ ¾ in pieces. Place in a saucepan over medium heat and cook. Add the onions and sauté until the onions turn a golden colour. Pour the fat off the pan and add the flour. Cook gently for 1 minute. Add the tomato purée and red wine. Raise the heat and simmer for 5 minutes to reduce the wine. Pour in the brown stock and gently simmer, partially covered, for 30 minutes.

Hint *If using stock cubes, use half chicken stock and half beef stock. This will cut the rather strong salty flavour of a beef cube.*

Add the wine vinegar, salt and pepper. Taste for seasoning and add more if necessary.

To finish Purée in a food processor or pass through a food mill. Strain and adjust the seasoning if necessary.

To serve Serve in a sauce boat with the chosen meat.

SAUCE POIVRE VERT
Green Peppercorn Sauce

For grilled steak or breast of duck

This is one of the sauces that emerged from the new style of French cooking that began in the 1970s. Peppercorns that are picked when they are green are young and not yet ripe. They have a flavour that is milder and more delicate than black peppercorns which are left to ripen on the plant and then dry and blacken in the sun. Popular use of green peppercorns in the West has occurred in the last 30 years. They can be bought preserved in water or vinegar or dried. The ones packed in water are best for this recipe.

Cooking time: 25 minutes   To serve 6

INGREDIENTS	METRIC	IMPERIAL	AMERICAN
Dry white wine	225 ml	8 fl oz	1 cup
Armagnac or cognac	125 ml	4 fl oz	½ cup
Chicken stock	125 ml	4 fl oz	½ cup
Crème fraîche or double cream	90 ml	6 tbsp	6 tbsp
Unsalted butter	40 g	1½ oz	3 tbsp
Castor sugar	50 g	2 oz	¼ cup
Port	30 ml	2 tbsp	2 tbsp
Tinned green peppercorns, drained	15 g	½ oz	1 tbsp

Pour the white wine and armagnac into a small saucepan and bring to the boil. Let the liquid reduce by one third. Add the chicken stock and let reduce for 5 minutes. Add the *crème fraiche* and gently simmer for 10 minutes, stirring occasionally. Meanwhile, place the butter and sugar into a small pan and gently heat to melt both. Let cook until a light caramel colour. Add this to the reduced sauce and add the port. Mix well. Add the green peppercorns. Warm the sauce for 5 minutes.

Hint *Good quality green peppercorns are mild enough to eat whole. If you cannot find good ones, then make the sauce and strain the peppercorns out just before serving. The strong flavour will be there, and you won't spoil your sauce.*

To serve Spoon over duck or beef. The sauce can be made a few hours ahead and gently rewarmed.

SAUCE AUX CHAMPIGNONS ET AU PORTO

Mushroom and Port Sauce

For beef

This is one of my favourite sauces to make when we are having a very nice cut of steak grilled on a barbecue. It is quick, easy and blends perfectly with the barbecued flavour. For an extra treat, I sometimes add some wild mushrooms, either fresh or dried.

Cooking time: 15 minutes   To serve 6

INGREDIENTS	METRIC	IMPERIAL	AMERICAN
Unsalted butter	25 g	1 oz	2 tbsp
Mushrooms, sliced	225 g	8 oz	2 cups

Hint *Wild mushrooms such as cepes, morilles or chanterelle can be added to the recipe. Their flavour is so strong that only a few are needed to perfume the sauce, 25–50 g/ 1–2 oz/¼–½ cups for fresh ones, 15 g/½ oz/¼ cup for dried.*

Red port	225 ml	8 fl oz	1 cup
Crème fraîche or double cream	90 ml	6 tbsp	6 tbsp
Freshly ground nutmeg	1 tsp	1 tsp	1 tsp
Salt and freshly ground black pepper to taste			

Melt the butter in a saucepan and add the mushrooms. Dried mushrooms should be reconstituted in hot water to cover, before using. Toss them in the butter for 2 minutes or until they release their juice. Add the port and simmer for 5 minutes to reduce the liquor slightly. Add the *crème fraiche* and simmer for 5 more minutes. Add the nutmeg, salt and pepper and taste for seasoning. Add more if necessary.

To serve Carve the beef and spoon the sauce over, or pour the sauce into a sauce boat.

SAUCE CHASSEUR
Hunter's Sauce

For rabbit, small game, lamb, beef veal or chicken

La chasse (the French hunting season) conjures up images of the autumn. This sauce is a perfect accompaniment for this season. If you have some brown sauce in the freezer, then the addition of some mushrooms, shallots, white wine and tomatoes will produce a delicious sauce. The sauce can be made in advance and is usually served with a light meat such as veal, chicken or rabbit.

Cooking time: 25 minutes   To serve 6

INGREDIENTS	METRIC	IMPERIAL	AMERICAN
Unsalted butter	25 g	1 oz	2 tbsp
Shallots, finely chopped	2	2	2
Mushrooms, washed and sliced	225 g	8 oz	2 cups
Small tomatoes, skinned, quartered and seeded	4	4	4
Tomato purée	5 ml	1 tsp	1 tsp
Dry white wine	275 ml	½ pt	1¼ cups
Salt and freshly ground black pepper to taste			
Brown sauce (page 16) about	220–225 ml	7–8 fl oz	1 cup
TO GARNISH			
Fresh parsley, chopped	1 tbsp	1 tbsp	1 tbsp

Heat the butter in a frying pan and sauté the shallots until they are transparent. Add the mushrooms and gently sauté them until they are golden.

Hint *Toss the mushrooms lightly with a fork rather than stirring with a spoon. This will help to keep them whole.*

Add the tomatoes, tomato purée and white wine and simmer to reduce the liquid by about one half, about 5–10 minutes. Season with salt and pepper. Add the brown sauce and taste for seasoning, adding more if necessary.

You can deglaze the pan you have sautéed the meat in with a little water or white wine and add these juices to the sauce.

To serve Bring the sauce to a boil and serve over meat. Sprinkle chopped parsley on top to garnish.

SAUCE A LA ROMAINE
Romaine Sauce

For beef, tongue or venison

This is a sauce with a sweet and sour flavour produced by the addition of sugar and vinegar to a brown sauce. Garnished with sultanas, currants and toasted pine nuts, it has a definite Middle Eastern flavour. It can be prepared in advance and rewarmed. It is best to have some brown sauce in the freezer. The other ingredients are added quite easily.

Cooking time: 25 minutes   To serve 6

INGREDIENTS	METRIC	IMPERIAL	AMERICAN
Castor sugar	25 g	2 tbsp	2 tbsp
Red wine vinegar	50 ml	2 fl oz	¼ cup
Brown sauce (page 16)	275 ml	½ pt	1¼ cups
Pine nuts, grilled	30 g	2 tbsp	2 tbsp
Sultanas, washed and drained	15 g	1 tbsp	1 tbsp
Currants, washed and drained	15 g	1 tbsp	1 tbsp
Salt and freshly ground black pepper to taste			

Melt the sugar in a heavy-bottomed saucepan and cook it until it starts to caramalise or turn a golden colour. Take it off the heat and add the vinegar.

Hint The caramel may spatter when the vinegar is added so be sure to remove it from the heat and protect your hand with an oven glove.

Add the brown sauce and gently cook until all the caramel is melted. Cook for about 10 minutes or until the liquid is reduced by about a quarter. Place the pine nuts under the grill and toast them until they are slightly golden. Add them to the sauce. Add the sultanas and currants. Taste for seasoning and add salt and pepper as needed.

If making the sauce in advance, then add the pine nuts, sultanas and currants to the sauce a few minutes before serving.

To serve Serve the warm sauce over the meat.

SAUCE ROBERT
Brown Sauce with Mustard

For pork, beef, grilled chicken or turkey

This is beautiful rich sauce with a tangy mustard flavour which gives the sauce body. It is a sauce built on a brown sauce, so if you have some made and frozen, the recipe can be produced very quickly.

Cooking time: 40 minutes   To serve 6

INGREDIENTS	METRIC	IMPERIAL	AMERICAN
Unsalted butter	25 g	1 oz	2 tbsp
Onion, finely chopped	25 g	1 oz	2 tbsp
Dry white wine or dry vermouth	175 ml	6 fl oz	¾ cup
Brown sauce (page 16)	425 ml	¾ pt	2 cups
Dijon mustard	45 ml	3 tbsp	3 tbsp
Unsalted butter, softened	40 g	1½ oz	3 tbsp
Salt and freshly ground black pepper to taste			
Fresh parsley, chopped	2 tbsp	2 tbsp	2 tbsp

Melt the butter in a saucepan and add the onion. Cook gently for 10 minutes until transparent. Add the white wine and raise the heat. Reduce the wine to about 30–45 ml/2–3 tbsp. Add the brown sauce and simmer gently for 10 minutes. The recipe can be made ahead to this point.

Hint If the sauce becomes too thick on standing, thin with a little brown stock.

To finish Cream the mustard and butter together. Just before serving take off the heat and whisk in the mustard and butter. Taste for seasoning. Add salt, pepper and parsley.

To serve Serve with meat.

SAUCE DIABLE
Devil Sauce

For grilled meats: chicken, pork or beef

The spice for this 'sauce of the devil' is black pepper. It is built on a brown sauce, so if you have some in your freezer, the sauce can be made in minutes.

Cooking time: 15 minutes   To serve 6

INGREDIENTS	METRIC	IMPERIAL	AMERICAN
Unsalted butter	25 g	1 oz	2 tbsp
Shallots, finely chopped	25 g	2 tbsp	2 tbsp
Dry vermouth	225ml	8 fl oz	1 cup
Brown sauce (page 16)	425 ml	¾ pt	2 cups
Crushed black peppercorns	15	15	15
Salt to taste			
Fresh parsley, finely chopped	1 tbsp	1 tbsp	1 tbsp

Melt the butter in a saucepan and add the shallots. Sauté for 3–5 minutes until the shallots are transparent. Add the vermouth and bring to the boil. Reduce the liquid until there are 15–30 ml/1–2 tablespoonfuls left. Add the brown sauce and the pepper. Simmer for 2–3 minutes. Strain. If you like a very peppery sauce, then do not strain it. The sauce can be made ahead and gently rewarmed when needed. Taste for seasoning and add salt if necessary.

To serve Add the chopped parsley and serve in a sauce boat or spooned over the meat.

SAUCE BORDELAISE
Red Wine Sauce

For steak, kidneys or eggs

Beef marrow, *moelle*, is a delicacy in France. It is the spongy centre of a marrow bone. This juicy morsel is added to a reduction of red wine and brown sauce to form one of France's best known sauces.

Cooking time: 25 minutes   To serve 6

INGREDIENTS	METRIC	IMPERIAL	AMERICAN
Shallots, finely chopped	25 g	2 tbsp	2 tbsp
Red wine	150 ml	¼ pt	⅔ cup
Brown sauce (page 16)	275 ml	½ pt	1¼ cups
Beef marrow, cut in small cubes	50 g	2 oz	¼ cup
Salt and freshly ground black pepper to taste			
Fresh parsley, chopped	1 tbsp	1 tbsp	1 tbsp

Hint *Preparing marrow is very easy. Ask your butcher for a good marrow bone. Be sure that he cracks it open for you. All you need do then is remove the marrow from the bone and cut it into cubes.*

Place the shallots and wine in a saucepan and bring to the boil. Reduce the liquid by one half. Add the brown sauce and continue to simmer for about 10 minutes. The sauce can be made in advance to this point. Just before serving, place the beef marrow into a pot of warm water and simmer for 3–4 minutes until it turns opaque. Add to the sauce. Add salt and pepper to taste. The sauce may thicken considerably if it stands. This is due to the marrow. Simply add more stock or water to thin.

To serve Sprinkle the sauce with the chopped parsley. Serve in a sauce boat or spooned over the meat.

SAUCE FROIDE AU RAIFORT
Cold Horseradish Sauce

For boiled beef, cold meats, or fish

A cold horseradish sauce is a wonderful accompaniment to cold meats as well as to traditional roast beef. As with the warm horseradish sauce, fresh horseradish does make a difference. It's worth the effort to find it.

Preparation time: 5 minutes   To serve 6

INGREDIENTS	METRIC	IMPERIAL	AMERICAN
Horseradish, grated	50 g	2 oz	¼ cup
OR Bottled horseradish (not creamed)	50 g	2 oz	¼ cup
Dijon mustard	2.5 ml	½ tsp	½ tsp
White wine vinegar or lemon juice	15 ml	1 tbsp	1 tbsp
Castor sugar	1 tsp	1 tsp	1 tsp
Soured cream	175 ml	6 fl oz	¾ cup
Salt and freshly ground white pepper			

Mix the horseradish, mustard, vinegar and sugar together. Pour the soured cream over the mixture and blend well. Taste for seasoning and add salt and pepper as needed.

Hint *If using bottled horseradish, you may wish to add more vinegar or lemon juice. Taste to determine if this is necessary. If using dehydrated horseradish, then make the sauce in advance so the flakes can reconstitute. Add a little milk or cream if the sauce becomes too thick.*

To serve Serve in a sauce boat with the meat.

SAUCE CHAUDE AU RAIFORT

Warm Horseradish Sauce

For boiled or roast beef

Chaucer once wrote, 'Woe to the cook whose sauce had no sting.' I suspect in his day a good strong sauce was needed to cover rotten or stale meat. Today, although our meat is of a better quality, we still enjoy a sauce with a bite. It is especially good with boiled meats. Fresh horseradish really gives this sauce a special flavour. However, bottled horseradish can be used with a milder result.

Cooking time: 20 minutes   To serve 6

INGREDIENTS	METRIC	IMPERIAL	AMERICAN
Unsalted butter	25 g	1 oz	¼ cup
Plain flour	25 g	1 oz	2 tbsp
Freshly grated horseradish	100 g	4 oz	1 cup
OR Bottled horseradish (not creamed)	100 g	4 oz	1 cup
Brown stock (page 12)	225 ml	8 fl oz	1 cup
White wine vinegar	5 ml	1 tsp	1 tsp
Dijon mustard	5 ml	1 tsp	1 tsp
Double cream	175 ml	6 fl oz	¾ cup
Salt and freshly ground black pepper to taste			

Hint *If you do not have a good brown stock, then use chicken stock rather than a beef cube. The prepared beef cubes tend to be too salty.*

Melt the butter in a saucepan and add the flour. Stir the flour over a low heat until it turns a light brown or café au lait colour. Mix in the horseradish.

Hint *If using a dehydrated horseradish, more stock will be needed. The dried flakes will absorb the liquid.*

Add the stock little by little to form a smooth sauce. Bring the sauce to a boil and lower the heat. Simmer for 5 minutes to cook the flour. Add the remaining ingredients and taste for seasoning. Add more if necessary.

If made in advance, leave out the cream and add it just before serving. Note that the horseradish will lose some of its bite if it sits too long.

To serve Serve immediately in a sauce boat.

ROND DE GIGOT AU PORTO

Leg of Lamb Steak with Port Wine Sauce

For lamb steaks or chops

Lamb steaks are now readily available. They can be cooked rare or well done to suit all tastes and make a welcome alternative to regular steaks. This is a simple yet elegant recipe. The entire recipe can be made in minutes.

Cooking time: 35 minutes   To serve 6

INGREDIENTS	METRIC	IMPERIAL	AMERICAN
Unsalted butter	25 g	1 oz	2 tbsp
Vegetable oil	15 ml	1 tbsp	1 tbsp
Steaks cut from a leg of lamb	6	6	6

Hint *Ask your butcher to cut the steaks vertically through the leg of lamb. This will give you a round steak with a circle of bone in the centre.*

Salt and freshly ground black pepper to taste			
Shallots, finely chopped	2	2	2
Port wine	75 ml	3 fl oz	6 tbsp
Brown stock (page 12)	175 ml	6 fl oz	¾ cup
Crème fraîche or double cream	90 ml	6 tbsp	6 tbsp

Place the butter and oil in a large heavy-bottomed frying pan. When the pan is very hot and the fat is sizzling, add one lamb steak to the pan. Move it in the pan to keep it from sticking to the bottom. Cook for 2 minutes and turn. Salt and pepper the cooked side. Cook for another 2 minutes and remove to a warm platter. Continue cooking the steaks in this manner until all the steaks are browned.

Hint *The steaks will be rare. If you like your lamb more well done, then cook them longer.*

Cover the steaks to keep them warm. Pour off any excess fat.

Hint *If you have burned the fat in the pan during the browning, then rinse the pan and add more fat. The burned bits will give the sauce a bitter flavour.*

Lower the heat and add the shallots to the pan. Cook until transparent. Deglaze the pan with the port, scraping up all the browned bits on the bottom. Add the brown stock and reduce the liquid by about half. Add the *crème fraîche*, and salt and pepper to taste.

To serve Strain the sauce into a sauce boat and spoon over the lamb steaks.

SAUCE AUX PRUNEAUX
Prune Sauce

For pork

Dried red or purple plums have been used for centuries. In France the most renowned varieties come from Agen and Touraine. Prunes poached in port take on a rich flavour that make this a sauce that enhances a meat such as pork. This sauce will keep several days in the refrigerator.

Cooking time: 30 minutes   To serve 6

INGREDIENTS	METRIC	IMPERIAL	AMERICAN
Prunes (stoned if possible)	175 g	6 oz	6 oz
Water to cover prunes			
Tea bag	1	1	1
Port	275 ml	½ pt	1¼ cups
Brown stock	275 ml	½ pt	1¼ cups
Juice and zest (grated rind) of lemon	1	1	1
Ground cinnamon	1 tsp	1 tsp	1 tsp
Salt and freshly ground black pepper to taste			

Place the prunes in a pan, cover with water and add the tea bag.

Hint *Using a tea bag will help to keep the deep colour in the prunes*

Bring the water to a simmer and remove from the heat. Let the prunes soak for several hours or overnight. Drain the prunes and stone if necessary. The water and tea bag can be discarded. Place in a pan with the port. Bring to a simmer and cook for 20 minutes. The prunes should be plump and soft. Drain them and reserve the liquid. Purée the prunes. This can be done in a food processor or liquidiser. Place back on the heat and add the reserved port and stock little by little, stirring constantly to form a sauce. Add the lemon zest and cinnamon. Bring to a simmer and add half the lemon juice and salt and pepper. Taste for seasoning. Add more lemon juice, salt and pepper as necessary. This sauce can be made a day ahead and rewarmed.

To serve Serve spooned over roasted or grilled pork, or in a sauce boat.

Les Sauces pour les Légumes

SAUCES FOR VEGETABLES

Here are a few ideas to add flavour to your vegetables. Garden fresh vegetables are an important part of any meal. Not very long ago we had a choice of cauliflower, Brussels sprouts or some frozen peas as our winter selection of vegetables. Now we have an excellent choice, many flown in from various parts of the globe. With this as inspiration, it is fun to create dishes that build on the crisp texture, garden freshness and flavour through the use of herbs or other ingredients. You will find that these blend or even contrast with the vegetables. I have included a few ideas to turn an accompanying vegetable into a dish with its own merit. Try a well-seasoned Mornay Sauce with broccoli or cauliflower. Or an Onion Cream or Bacon Sauce when serving crisp green beans or mangetouts.

Herbed butters can be made in advance and kept in the refrigerator or frozen. They can impart the flavour of fresh dill, mint or tarragon, and can provide a pleasant surprise when these herbs are not in season. Steam fresh vegetables and pour some melted herbed butter over them for a quick way to dress up your vegetables.

SAUCE MORNAY
Cheese Sauce

For vegetables, eggs, fish or poultry

The addition of cheese and spices transforms a basic bechamel into a rich cheese sauce. *Gratinéed* dishes are made by pouring Mornay Sauce over the food and sprinkling cheese on top. The dish is placed under a grill to brown.

Hint *If too much cheese is used, the sauce will become stringy.*

Cooking time: 5 minutes   To serve 6

INGREDIENTS	METRIC	IMPERIAL	AMERICAN
Bechamel sauce (page 14)	275 ml	½ pt	1¼ cups
Gruyère cheese, grated (or Cheddar)	25 g	1 oz	¼ cup
Parmesan cheese, freshly grated	25 g	1 oz	2 tbsp
Pinch of cayenne			
Salt and freshly ground white pepper			
Unsalted butter (optional)	25 g	1 oz	2 tbsp

Hint *If using this sauce for a gratin, omit the butter enrichment, make it thinner, and use less cheese.*

Warm the bechamel sauce. If it is very thick, add a little warm milk. Stir in the grated cheese. Add cayenne, salt and pepper to taste. Blend until all the cheese is melted.

To finish Just before serving whisk in the butter (optional). This can be made a day in advance.

Hint *If you are not going to use the sauce immediately, place a piece of plastic wrap or buttered greaseproof paper over the top of* the sauce to stop a skin forming. Or gently pour some melted butter over the top to seal the sauce. When you are ready to use the sauce either remove the cover or warm the sauce and stir in the butter.

The sauce may thicken on standing. If it becomes too thick, then add a little more tepid milk to reach the desired consistency.

SAUCE A LA MOUTARDE
Mustard Sauce

For vegetables, warmed sausages, ham, grilled fish or boiled eggs

This piquant mustard sauce is one of several variations to a basic béchamel or white sauce. It can be made ahead and gently rewarmed.

Cooking time: 5 minutes   To serve 6

INGREDIENTS	METRIC	IMPERIAL	AMERICAN
Béchamel sauce (page 14)	275 ml	½ pt	1¼ cups
Dijon mustard	15 ml	1 tbsp	1 tbsp
Moutarde de Meaux (or coarse grained mustard)	15 ml	1 tbsp	1 tbsp
White wine vinegar	15 ml	1 tbsp	1 tbsp
Salt and freshly ground white pepper to taste			

Warm the bechamel sauce. If it is too thick, add a little warm milk. Add the mustards and wine vinegar. Mix in well. Season with salt and pepper. Taste. If a sharper flavour is desired, add more mustard and a drop of vinegar.

If made in advance, place a piece of plastic wrap or buttered greaseproof paper over the top of the sauce to stop a skin forming. Or gently pour some melted butter over the top to seal the sauce. When you are ready to use the sauce, either remove the cover or warm the sauce and stir in the butter.

Hint *The sauce may thicken on standing. If it becomes too thick, add a little more tepid milk to reach the desired consistency and taste. Correct the seasoning if necessary.*

To serve Serve warm, spooned over the vegetables or chosen dish.

SAUCE AUX OIGNONS ET A LA CREME FRAICHE
Onion Cream Sauce

For cooked vegetables

Make this sauce while your vegetables are steaming or boiling. Then turn the vegetables in the sauce and serve. The secret of this sauce is the slow careful cooking of the onions. They should be sautéed to a sweet, golden brown, not burned. Sweating the onions, as described in the glossary, is a perfect way to achieve this result. The onions do not have to be constantly watched using this method.

Cooking time: 35 minutes   To serve 6

INGREDIENTS	METRIC	IMPERIAL	AMERICAN
Unsalted butter	25 g	1 oz	2 tbsp
Large onion, chopped	1	1	1
Crème fraîche (or soured cream)	225 ml	8 fl oz	1 cup
Salt and freshly ground white pepper to taste			

Melt the butter in a frying pan and sauté the onion until a rich golden colour. This should be done over a gentle heat and will take about 30 minutes. Do not let the onion burn. Remove from the heat and stir in the cream. Warm through and add salt and pepper to taste.

To finish Cook the vegetables to be served, and when ready add them to the cream sauce in the pan. Turn them in the sauce and serve immediately.

SAUCE A LA POITRINE FUME
— Bacon Sauce —
For green vegetables
(especially cooked green beans)

Blanch tender young green beans and then sauté them in butter. Pour some of this mildly sweet and sour sauce over them and serve. This sauce can be made ahead and warmed when needed.

Cooking time: 20 minutes   To serve 6

INGREDIENTS	METRIC	IMPERIAL	AMERICAN
Smoked streaky bacon, rind removed, coarsely diced	100 g	4 oz	4 oz
Unsalted butter	50 g	2 oz	¼ cup
Shallots, chopped	3	3	3
Plain flour	20 g	¾ oz	2 tbsp
Chicken stock	275 ml	½ pt	1¼ cups
White wine vinegar	30 ml	2 tbsp	2 tbsp
Castor sugar	25 g	1 oz	2 tbsp
Salt and freshly ground black pepper to taste			

Place the bacon in a pan and gently cook until crisp. Remove the bacon and drain on kitchen towel. Pour off the fat. Melt half the butter and add the shallots. Cook until tender. Remove the shallots. Melt the rest of the butter and add the flour to make a roux. Cook for one minute without colouring. Pour in the chicken stock little by little to form a sauce. Add the vinegar and sugar. Simmer for 2–3 minutes. Add the bacon and shallots. Add salt and pepper to taste. Be careful not to add too much salt. The bacon is already salty. Add more vinegar or sugar as needed.

The sauce can be made a few hours in advance and may thicken on standing. If this occurs, thin with warm stock.

To serve Pour over cooked vegetables.

ARTICHAUTS A LA SAUCE AU CITRON
— Artichokes with Lemon Sauce —
For any green vegetables

A large pot filled with artichokes sprinkled with lemon quarters is so attractive that I would almost rather take a picture than cook them! This is a delicious way to serve artichokes. The tart sauce can be served with other vegetables as well.

Cooking time: 45 minutes   To serve 6

INGREDIENTS	METRIC	IMPERIAL	AMERICAN
Artichokes	6	6	6
Lemon, quartered	1	1	1
Bay leaves	2	2	2
Water	1.7 l	3 pt	1¾ qt
FOR THE SAUCE			
Unsalted butter	100 g	4 oz	½ cup
Fresh lemon juice	50 ml	2 fl oz	¼ cup
Olive oil	50 ml	2 fl oz	¼ cup
Salt and freshly ground black pepper to taste			

Cut off the stem at the base of the artichokes. Cut about 2 cm/¼ in from the top of the artichokes. Take off any brown leaves. With scissors, cut the sharp points off of each leaf. Wash in cold salted water and drain. Place the prepared

Opposite: *Bombe Favorite* (page 91).

artichokes into a very large pot and pour in the water. Add the lemon quarters and bay leaves. Bring to the boil and cook for 30–40 minutes until the bases are tender. Do not overcook. If you do, the vegetables will not keep their shape when you remove the choke. Check during the cooking to see if more water is needed.

Meanwhile make the sauce. Melt the butter and mix in the lemon juice and olive oil. Add salt and pepper to taste.

To finish Open the leaves of the artichoke and remove the choke in the centre. Pour the lemon sauce into the centre.

Hint *The recipe can be made several hours ahead and refrigerated. To serve, rewarm the artichokes by steaming them over hot water until warmed through.*

To serve Serve extra sauce on the side for anyone who enjoys dipping the leaves in the sauce.

BEURRES COMPOSES
Cold Herbed Butters

For vegetables or meat

Whenever I see really beautiful fresh herbs in the market, I always buy them. Usually, I have more than I can possibly use while they're still fresh. This gives me a perfect opportunity to make herbed butters. If you have a food processor, this can be done in minutes and frozen. I freeze the butter in 225 g/8 oz packets and cut off a piece whenever I need it. All that needs to be done then is to pour some melted herbed butter (or place a pat) over your cooked vegetables or grilled meat. I have listed several types below, but you can easily lengthen this list by adding your own ideas.

BEURRE AUX ANCHOIS
Anchovy Butter

To make 225 g/8 oz

INGREDIENTS	METRIC	IMPERIAL	AMERICAN
Unsalted butter	100 g	4 oz	½ cup
Fillets of anchovy	6	6	6

Cream the butter. Pound the anchovies to a paste. Add to the butter and mix well. To be used with baked or grilled fish.

To store, wrap in foil and label. Freeze or place in the refrigerator.

Variations The anchovies can be substituted by cooked crayfish, cooked shrimp, cooked lobster, paprika or garlic.

Opposite: *Crêpes à la Crème Anglaise au Chocolat* (page 85).
Meringues à la Crème Anglaise (page 84).
Tartlettes aux Poires à la Crème Anglaise au Café (page 85).

BEURRE A L'ESTRAGON

Tarragon Butter

To make 225 g/8 oz

INGREDIENTS	METRIC	IMPERIAL	AMERICAN
Unsalted butter	225 g	8 oz	1 cup

Hint *If you prefer, substitute a good quality margarine for the butter. Unsalted margarine can now be found in some shops.*

Lemon juice	30 ml	2 tbsp	2 tbsp
Fresh tarragon, washed, dried and chopped	75 g	5 tbsp	5 tbsp
Salt and freshly ground black pepper to taste			

Soften the butter to room temperature. Cream it with a spoon or in a food processor or electric mixer. Add the lemon juice little by little. Mix in the herbs. Add salt and pepper to taste.

To store Wrap in foil and label. Freeze or place in the refrigerator.

Variations The tarragon can be substituted by dill, chives, parsley or a mixture of fresh herbs.

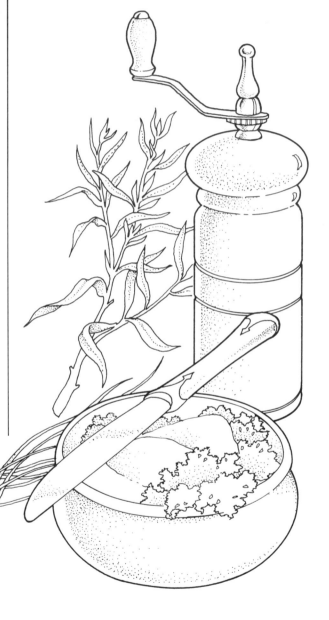

82

Les Sauces et les Crèmes pour les Entremets

DESSERT SAUCES

Sweet sauces add a crowning glory to one's meal. They are flavourful, luxurious and concentrated. One or two tablespoons per person is enough to bring out the essence of whatever dessert you have chosen.

Most sweet sauces can be divided into three major categories: custard or crème Anglaise, *fruit purées or sugar based sauces.*

Custard or crème Anglaise
Although vanilla is most often served, custard can be flavoured with chocolate, coffee, grand marnier or fruits. I once made an ice cream birthday cake with three different ice creams, decorated it with whipped cream, and served it as the centre piece of a dessert buffet table. It was surrounded by various custard sauces with their array of colours. Everyone had a choice of sauce. It provided a festive way to celebrate a birthday. Another dessert inspired by this lovely family of sauces is chocolate meringues sandwiched together with chocolate mousse, and served on a plate of chocolate custard. Sandwich the meringues together a day in advance so that they will soften slightly. This is a treat for your chocoholic friends.

Fruit purées
With the advent of lighter, fresher French cuisine, the fruit purées have come into their own. Raspberry, strawberry, blackcurrant or many combinations can be made. The ice cream bombé recipe makes a wonderful party dish. The bombé can be made well ahead and frozen and looks beautiful served with a raspberry purée. For Christmas I decorate the top of the bombé with fresh holly for a red and green treat.

Sugar based sauces
All dessert sauces have sugar as an essential ingredient, but there is a group of sauces that are based on the cooking of sugar alone, such as caramel sauce. The sauces can be made ahead and then poured over poached fruit or fresh peeled oranges. They have a lovely texture, and keep very well in the refrigerator. If friends drop by unexpectedly, you can warm some sauce and pour it over ice cream or cake and have an elegant sweet to serve.

CREME ANGLAISE
Custard Sauce

For fruit desserts, oeufs à la neige, ice cream, soufflés or any dessert where a sauce is desired

Knowing how to make a good custard sauce is important. Many sauces are built on it. With the addition of more eggs and cream a *Crème Anglaise* becomes the base for ice creams. With a little gelatine, whipped cream and flavouring it becomes a bavarian cream or *bavarois*.

The secret to a good custard is to patiently and slowly cook the sauce so that it thickens and does not curdle. It can be made in advance and will keep in the refrigerator for 3–4 days.

Cooking time: 20 minutes   To serve 6

INGREDIENTS	METRIC	IMPERIAL	AMERICAN
Milk	425 ml	¾ pt	2 cups
Castor sugar	75 g	3 oz	⅓ cup
Vanilla pod	1	1	1
Egg yolks (size 2)	4	4	4

Hint *Vanilla is the basic flavouring of this sauce. It is important to use good vanilla. Vanilla pods are sold in most food stores now. They can be rinsed and used 2–3 times.*

Place the milk, sugar and vanilla pod in a saucepan and warm until the sugar completely dissolves. Whisk the egg yolks in a bowl and very slowly pour in the milk, whisking constantly.

Hint *Pour a few drops of milk into the egg mixture and stir. Then add a few more drops. This way you will be warming the yolks slowly and there will be less chance of curdling.*

When all the milk has been incorporated into the eggs, place the mixture back in the saucepan and heat over a low heat, stirring constantly, until the cream thickens. This will take at least 15 minutes or longer.

Hint *I place a pan of cold water next to the cooker. If I find that the sauce is starting to curdle, then I quickly place the saucepan into the cold water and stir. This will stop the cooking immediately.*

When the sauce coats the back of a spoon, it is ready. A simple test is to dip a spoon in the sauce and draw your finger across the back of it. If a clear line remains, then the sauce is ready. Strain the sauce into a bowl and continue to stir until it cools. This is important. Many sauces are spoiled at this point. The sauce is still hot when taken from the heat and can curdle.

To serve Serve at room temperature.

The following variations illustrate how the basic sauce can be built upon to provide a wide range of flavourful sauces. For example, make *Crème Anglaise à la Liqueur* by adding 15 ml/1 tbsp of kirsch, cognac, orange liqueur or other liqueur to a cool *Crème Anglaise*.

CREME ANGLAISE AU CHOCOLAT
Chocolate Custard Sauce

**Cooking time: 25 minutes
To make 425 ml/¾ pt/2 cups**

INGREDIENTS	METRIC	IMPERIAL	AMERICAN
Semi-sweet chocolate	100 g	4 oz	4 oz
Milk	425 ml	¾ pt	2 cups
Castor sugar	75 g	3 oz	⅓ cup
Vanilla pod	1	1	1
Egg yolks (size 2)	4	4	4

Break the chocolate into pieces and place in a saucepan. Place the saucepan in a bain marie and gently melt the chocolate.

Hint *Chocolate melts beautifully in a microwave. It should take about 2 minutes depending on the type of machine you have.*

Heat the milk, sugar and vanilla pod as in the basic recipe and, when the sugar has dissolved, pour very slowly into the melted chocolate, stirring constantly. Place the chocolate mixture on the heat and blend thoroughly. Whisk the egg yolks in a bowl and proceed with the recipe as above, slowly adding the chocolate milk mixture to the eggs. Continue as above.

Hint *This sauce is delicious poured over rolled crêpes filled with cream or ice cream.*

MERINGUES AU CHOCOLAT A LA CREME ANGLAISE

Chocolate Meringues with Custard Sauce

INGREDIENTS	METRIC	IMPERIAL	AMERICAN
FOR THE MERINGUES			
Icing sugar	75 g	3 oz	⅓ cup
Cocoa powder	20 g	¾ oz	1 tbsp
Egg whites	3	3	3
Castor sugar	75 g	3 oz	3 oz
FOR THE CHOCOLATE MOUSSE			
Chocolate	100 g	4 oz	½ cup
Unsalted butter	50 g	2 oz	¼ cup
Egg yolks	2	2	2
Egg whites	3	3	3
Castor sugar	20 g	¾ oz	1 tbsp
Icing sugar	50 g	2 oz	¼ cup

To make the meringues, mix the icing sugar and cocoa powder. Beat the egg whites to a stiff peak, add 1 tsp of the castor sugar and beat for 10 seconds. When the whites are stiff, add the rest of the castor sugar and beat. Quickly fold in the cocoa and icing sugar mixture and pipe in the shape of small disks onto a greased baking sheet. Bake at 130°C/250°F/gas mark ½ for about 40 minutes or until they are completely dried out.

To make the mousse, melt the chocolate and add the butter, softened to room temperature. Mix the egg yolks together and add to the slightly cooled chocolate. Beat the egg whites to stiff peaks, add 1 tsp of sugar and beat again. Fold in the rest of the sugar. Beat a large spoonful of the whites into the cooled chocolate mixture to soften it. Fold the chocolate mixture into the egg whites.

To serve Sandwich the meringues together with a spoonful of the chocolate mousse and pipe some mousse on top. For each serving pour a little *Crème Anglaise* onto a plate and place a meringue on top.

CREME ANGLAISE AU CAFE

Coffee Custard Sauce

Cooking time: 20 minutes
To make 425 ml/¾ pt/2 cups

INGREDIENTS	METRIC	IMPERIAL	AMERICAN
Instant coffee	1 tbsp	1 tbsp	1 tbsp
Milk	425 ml	¾ pt	2 cups
Castor sugar	75 g	3 oz	⅓ cup
Vanilla pod	1	1	1
Egg yolks (size 2)	4	4	4

Dissolve the coffee in the milk with the sugar and vanilla. Proceed with the basic recipe as above.

85

CRÈME ANGLAISE AU CARAMEL
Caramel Custard Sauce

Cooking time: 30 minutes
To make 425 ml/¾ pt/2 cups

INGREDIENTS	METRIC	IMPERIAL	AMERICAN
Milk	425 g	¾ pt	2 cups
Sugar cubes	150 g	5 oz	5 oz
Water to moisten each cube plus	15 ml	1 tbsp	1 tbsp
Egg yolks (size 2)	4	4	4

Place sugar cubes in a heavy-bottomed saucepan and moisten with water. Add the extra water. Dissolve the sugar over a low heat. Do not let the liquid boil until all the sugar is completely dissolved.

Once the sugar is dissolved and the liquid looks clear, bring the liquid to the boil and cook until it is a light caramel colour. Take off the heat and slowly pour the milk into the caramel. Cover your hand with an oven glove. The caramel will spatter when the milk is poured in. Place over the heat to completely dissolve any hardened sugar. Proceed as for the basic custard recipe, pouring the caramel flavoured milk slowly into the eggs.

This sauce is delicious with pear tarts. Line tartlet tins with shortcrust pastry and bake blind. Peel, halve and core 3 ripe pears. Dissolve 100 g/4 oz/½ cup of sugar in 50 ml/2 fl oz/¼ cup of water and boil to a light caramel colour. Add the pears, cover and poach until soft, 3–4 minutes. Slice the pears into the tarts and spoon the caramel over and around them.

SAUCE AU CHOCOLAT
Chocolate Sauce

For ice cream, mousses, poached pears, or profiteroles

Chocolate sauce should be dark, sweet, rich and full of chocolate flavour. The sauce should be simmered for some time so that the consistency becomes thick and creamy without the use of cornflour.

Cooking time: 20 minutes   To serve 6

INGREDIENTS	METRIC	IMPERIAL	AMERICAN
Good quality semi-sweet chocolate	200 g	7 oz	7 oz
Castor sugar	100 g	4 oz	½ cup
Water	200 ml	7 fl oz	scant cup
Rum	15 ml	1 tbsp	1 tbsp
OR vanilla pod	1	1	1

Break the chocolate into small pieces and place in a heavy-bottomed saucepan with the sugar and water. Melt the chocolate over a low heat. If using a vanilla pod, put it in with the chocolate. If using rum, mix it in when the sauce is finished. When the chocolate is melted and the sugar dissolved, mix well. Bring the sauce to a simmer and simmer gently for 10–15 minutes or until thickened.

Hint *Do not let the sauce boil rapidly. The cocoa fats will separate and the sugar will crystalise.*

Pour into a sauce boat and cool. It will keep in the refrigerator for at least a week.

To serve Gently warm the sauce before serving.

SAUCE AU CHOCOLAT AMER

Bitter Chocolate Sauce

For ice creams, mousses, poached pears, or profiteroles

This is a rich chocolate sauce made with cream and milk. It glistens as it pours. Try to buy the best bitter chocolate you can find. It is sometimes called 'dry chocolate'.

Cooking time: 15 minutes   To serve 6

INGREDIENTS	METRIC	IMPERIAL	AMERICAN
Bitter chocolate	100 g	4 oz	4 oz
Milk	90 ml	6 tbsp	6 tbsp
Double cream	30 ml	2 tbsp	2 tbsp
Unsalted butter	15 g	½ oz	1 tbsp
Castor sugar	25 g	1 oz	2 tbsp

Break up the chocolate into pieces and place in a saucepan. Place the saucepan in a bain marie and gently melt the chocolate.

Hint *Chocolate melts beautifully in a microwave. It should take about 2 minutes depending on the type of machine you have.*

Meanwhile put the milk, cream, butter and sugar into a saucepan and bring to the simmer. Add to the melted chocolate little by little, mixing well. When the chocolate is thoroughly mixed, place back on the heat and bring to a boil. Pour into a bowl to cool, stirring occasionally.

SAUCE AU CHOCOLAT FONDANT

Chocolate Fudge Sauce

For ice creams or rich cakes

For those who enjoy rich, fudgy sauces, their dream can be realised by the addition of golden syrup to a chocolate sauce. It turns to a glaze when poured over ice cream.

Cooking time: 15 minutes   To serve 6

INGREDIENTS	METRIC	IMPERIAL	AMERICAN
Bitter or dry chocolate	100 g	4 oz	4 oz
Unsalted butter, softened	50 g	2 oz	¼ cup
Water	175 ml	6 fl oz	¾ cup
Castor sugar	225 g	8 oz	1 cup
Golden syrup	90 ml	6 tbsp	6 tbsp

Melt the chocolate in a saucepan over a low heat.

Hint *Chocolate melts beautifully in a microwave. It should take about 2 minutes depending on the type of machine you have.*

Mix in the butter. Add the water and mix thoroughly. Add the sugar and golden syrup. Bring to a boil and gently simmer for about 10 minutes or until thick. If it is thin, let it simmer gently until thickened. As it cools it will continue to thicken. It can be gently rewarmed before serving.

To serve Serve warm over ice cream or cake.

Sauce au Caramel
Caramel Sauce

For citrus fruits, poached fruits, ice cream or bavarian cream

The sparkling, golden colour of this sauce combined with orange sections or poached fruit is very pretty. It is especially attractive served in a glass dish or bowl. The sauce can be made a week ahead and kept tightly covered in the refrigerator.

Cooking time: 20 minutes   To serve 6

INGREDIENTS	METRIC	IMPERIAL	AMERICAN
Granulated or castor sugar	250 g	9 oz	1¼ cups
Cold water	200 ml	7 fl oz	scant cup
Warm water	350 ml	12 fl oz	1½ cups

Place the sugar and cold water in a heavy-bottomed saucepan and heat gently to completely dissolve the sugar. Be careful not to let the water boil until all the sugar is dissolved.

Hint *If the water starts to boil while there are still granules of sugar, these granules will start to burn before the syrup caramalises. It will give a grainy and bitter taste to the sauce.*

Once the sugar is dissolved and the liquid looks clear, bring the syrup to a boil and continue a rapid boil until it starts to turn a caramel or golden colour. This can take 10 minutes. When it reaches this colour, quickly dip the saucepan into a basin of cold water to stop the cooking. Cover your hand with an oven glove and pour in the warm water. The syrup may spatter and it is wise to protect your hand. Replace on a low heat to dissolve any hardened caramel. Cool the sauce and serve, or cover and refrigerate.

Sauce au Caramel et a la Creme Fraiche
Cream Caramel Sauce

For ice creams, sundaes, or poached fruit such as pears and apples

This is a creamy alternative to a simple caramel sauce. It is very similar in taste to butterscotch. The rich smooth texture allows the sauce to cling to fruits or gives body to an ice cream sundae.

Cooking time: 20 minutes   To serve 6

INGREDIENTS	METRIC	IMPERIAL	AMERICAN
Granulated or castor sugar	175 g	6 oz	¾ cup
Water	150 ml	¼ pt	⅔ cup
Double cream	175 ml	6 fl oz	¾ cup
Milk (if needed)	125 ml	4 fl oz	½ cup

Place the sugar and water into a heavy-bottomed saucepan and heat gently to completely dissolve the sugar. Be careful not to let the water boil until all the sugar is dissolved.

Hint *If the water starts to boil while there are still granules of sugar, these granules will start to burn before the syrup caramalises. It will give a grainy and bitter taste to the sauce.*

Once the sugar is dissolved and the liquid looks clear, bring the syrup to a boil and continue a rapid boil until it starts to turn a caramel or golden colour. This can take 10 minutes. Leave to cool for 3–4 minutes. Meanwhile, place the cream in a saucepan and bring it to a boil. Stir it into the caramel a little at a time. Replace the pan over a low heat to melt any hardened caramel. When the sauce is smooth, it is ready to serve as a warm sauce.

Hint *The sauce will thicken as it cools. To thin it, bring the milk to a boil and let it cool. Stir it into the sauce.*

It will keep 3–4 days in the refrigerator.

To serve The sauce can be served slightly warm or at room temperature, or it can be heated and served hot. It forms a nice contrast over cold ice cream or fruit.

CRÈME A L'ORANGE
— *Orange Cream Sauce* —

For fruit, ice creams or plain cakes

As with a custard sauce, this sauce is thickened with eggs. It has such a refreshing flavour that I enjoy serving it on its own in little *pots de crème*. These are pretty little pots which are usually used for chocolate creams or mousses. Ramekins or even pretty demi-tasse cups could be used.

Cooking time: 20 minutes   To serve 6

INGREDIENTS	METRIC	IMPERIAL	AMERICAN
Large oranges, juice and zest (grated rind)	3	3	3
Small lemon, juice and zest	1	1	1
Castor sugar	50 g	2 oz	¼ cup
Eggs	3	3	3
Double cream	45 ml	3 tbsp	3 tbsp
Kirsch	15 ml	1 tbsp	1 tbsp

Grate the rind of the oranges and lemon into a stainless steel or enamelled pan. Add the juice from the fruit, the sugar and eggs. Mix these ingredients together and place over a low heat.

Hint *It is important to use a stainless steel pan and spoon, a wooden spoon or a stainless steel whisk. If an aluminium pot and whisk are used together, the acid in the sauce will react with the metal and the sauce will turn grey. Many old cookbooks mention using a silver spoon to stir some sauces. This was before the days of stainless steel.*

Cook gently, stirring constantly, until the cream thickens. It will coat the back of a spoon. A simple test is to dip a spoon into the sauce and draw your finger across the back of it. If a clear line remains, then the sauce is ready. Pour it into a bowl and continue to stir until it cools. This is important. The sauce will continue to cook in its own heat and will curdle if allowed to sit in the bowl. Half whip the cream.

Hint *To half whip cream means to whip it until it is the same consistency as the orange cream. It will blend in better this way.*

When the sauce is completely cooled, add the crown and ikirsch. Fold in well.

To serve Pour into individual pots or serve as a sauce from a sauce boat.

COULIS DE FRUITS
Fruit Sauces

Fruit sauces are colourful, light and delicious. It is interesting that nouvelle cuisine has emphasised purées to which the name *coulis* has been given. The name was used by Taillevent in the fourteenth century, and later by La Varenne, Menon and Careme. The term *coulis* (or cullis) meant a sauce. More precisely, it was the name for the juice which runs out of meat when cooking. More restrictive definitions were also used, but not until recently was the term applied to fruit purées.

Berries work best, but it is fun to experiment with your favourite fruit. The sugar content will vary with the fruit. Use 1 part sugar to 3 parts fruit as a good guide. A liqueur can be added or not. Choose a liqueur that complements the fruit. As an example, when serving a blackberry coulis, I sometimes use Crème de Casis.

COULIS DE FRAMBOISES
Raspberry Sauce

For crêpes, bavarois, meringue glacé, fresh fruit, ice cream, sorbet or cake

The bright red colour of this fruit sauce makes it a pretty accompaniment to any dessert. The fruit should be ripe. If it is not in season, then use good quality frozen raspberries.

Preparation time: 10 minutes   To serve 6

INGREDIENTS	METRIC	IMPERIAL	AMERICAN
Raspberries, washed and hulled if fresh, defrosted if frozen	250 g	9 oz	9 oz
Icing sugar	40 g	2½ oz	¼ cup + 1 tbsp
Kirsch	45 ml	3 tbsp	3 tbsp

Purée the raspberries either in a food processor, food mill or press through a sieve. Add the sugar and kirsch. The amount of sugar really depends on the ripeness of the raspberries. More sugar or kirsch may be necessary.

Hint *Be careful not to overpower the sauce with too much kirsch. It should lend a delicate flavour.*

Pass the sauce through a sieve to remove the pips. The sauce will keep for a week in the refrigerator. It may be frozen, but needs to be stirred while it is defrosting to bring it back to a smooth texture. If you have used frozen berries, then do not freeze again.

To serve Pour into a sauce boat and serve, or pour onto a plate and place fresh fruit, ice cream, sorbet or cake in the centre.

BOMBE FAVORITE
Ice Cream Bomb with Raspberry Sauce

Here is an easy recipe that you can prepare well in advance and freeze. The raspberry sauce is a perfect accompaniment for it. Ice cream bombs are always a favourite party dish. Originally 'bombs' were made in spherical moulds. Another reason they are called bombs is because there is a surprise inside. In this recipe there is a crunchy sweet centre that adds texture and flavour.

Cooking time: 50 minutes   To serve 6–8

INGREDIENTS	METRIC	IMPERIAL	AMERICAN
FOR THE MERINGUES			
Egg whites	2	2	2
Castor sugar	100 g	4 oz	½ cup
FOR THE ICE CREAM			
Double cream	275 ml	½ pt	1¼ cups
Vanilla sugar	40 g	3 tbsp	3 tbsp
FOR THE SAUCE			
Raspberry sauce (page 90)	275 ml	½ pt	1¼ cups

Hint *If you are in a hurry, buy meringues and carry on with the recipe*

To make the meringues Whisk the egg whites to a stiff peak, add 1 tsp of the sugar and continue beating for 10 seconds. Then quickly fold in the rest of the sugar. Work quickly and do not overfold the whites. The sugar will cause the whites to weep if overworked. Pipe or spoon the meringues onto a greased baking sheet or one lined with bakewell paper. Sprinkle them with some castor sugar. Heat the oven to 130°C/250°F/gas mark ½. Bake the meringues for about 40 minutes or until they are completely dried out.

To make the ice cream Whip the cream and add the sugar. If it is a warm day or your kitchen is warm, whip the cream in a bowl over another bowl filled with ice. This technique gives a lighter texture to your cream.

To finish Break up the meringues and fold them into the cream. Pour the cream and meringue mixture into a bombe mould or pudding basin. Cover with foil or plastic wrap and freeze for at least 2 hours. It will keep several weeks in the freezer.

To serve Take out of the freezer and leave in the refrigerator for about 30–45 minutes. The cream should still be firm, but not so hard that a knife won't cut it. Slip a palette knife around the inside of the mould to loosen the cream. Unmould onto a serving platter. Spoon the raspberry sauce over the top and let it run down the sides. Slice the ice cream and serve the rest of the sauce in a sauce boat.

SAUCE MONTMORENCY
Black Cherry Sauce

For ice cream

This sauce usually has dramatic overtones as it is served flambéed over vanilla ice cream. Here the cherries are marinated in the kirsch rather than flambéed in it. You can choose whichever method you prefer.

Cooking time: 10 minutes   To serve 6

INGREDIENTS	METRIC	IMPERIAL	AMERICAN
Pitted black cherries (tinned)	425 g	15 oz	2 cups
Kirsch	30 ml	2 tbsp	2 tbsp
Red currant jelly	100 g	4 oz	½ cup
Raspberries, puréed	100 g	4 oz	½ cup
Juice of orange	1	1	1
Fresh ginger, small slice			
Potato flour or cornflour	2 tsp	2 tsp	2 tsp

Drain the cherries and reserve the juice. Place the cherries in the kirsch to marinate.

Cream the redcurrant jelly by mixing it until it is smooth. Add all but 30 ml/2 tbsp of the reserved juice to the creamed jelly. Bring the juice and jelly to the boil. Simmer to melt the jelly. Add the raspberry purée, orange juice and ·piece of ginger and continue to simmer for 3–5 minutes. Do not boil. Remove the ginger. Mix the potato flour and remaining 30 ml/2 tbsp of juice together and add to the sauce. Simmer for 2 minutes or until the sauce thickens. Add the cherries and their marinade. This can be made ahead and rewarmed.

To serve Serve warm over ice cream.

SAUCE SABAYON
Sabayon Sauce

For sorbets, frozen soufflés, fresh fruit, or served warm on its own

This is a delicate sauce that is thickened by gently whisking egg yolks over heat. Very often it is made in a restaurant with great flourish at the table. When looking through antique shops, I love to see the old copper sabayon pots with their rounded bottoms made so that they could sit in a special bain marie. New ones are also available, but the old ones have a wonderful patina. The sauce is very delicate, and should only be made 30 minutes in advance, if served warm. If serving cold, it can be made a day ahead and kept covered in the refrigerator.

Cooking time: 15 minutes   To serve 6

INGREDIENTS	METRIC	IMPERIAL	AMERICAN
Egg yolks	5	5	5
Castor sugar	175 g	6 oz	¾ cup
Dry white wine, Sauternes, champagne, Marsala or sherry	225 ml	8 fl oz	1 cup

Hint *If an ordinary white wine is used, then a little grated lemon rind or a spoonful of vanilla sugar should be added with the yolks to give more flavour. If a better wine is used, this is not necessary.*

Place the egg yolks and sugar into a saucepan and hold over a bain marie or pan of water. The water should not touch the bottom of the saucepan. Bring the water to just below simmering. Whisk the mixture together until the sugar is completely dissolved. Do not let the water come to the boil or the eggs will curdle. Slowly pour in the wine, whisking constantly. The mixture will expand to nearly twice its volume in about 5 minutes. Continue to whisk for about another 5 minutes to make a thick, foamy sauce.

To serve cold Place the pan in a bowl of cold water and continue to whisk until it is cold. This is important. Once taken off the heat, the sauce will continue to cook in its own heat and curdle.

To serve warm Pour over sorbet, frozen soufflé, fresh fruit or into little individual bowls, and serve immediately.

SAUCE AUX ABRICOTS
Apricot Sauce

For custard desserts, sorbets or fruit

This sauce is thicker and sweeter than a fruit coulis. It is colourful and can be used where a heavier fruit sauce is desired.

Cooking time: 2 hours   To serve 6

INGREDIENTS	METRIC	IMPERIAL	AMERICAN
Dried apricots (Ripe, fresh ones are best, although good ones are difficult to find, even in season)	225 g	8 oz	8 oz
Castor sugar	100 g	4 oz	½ cup
Juice from orange	1	1	1
Juice from lemon	½	½	½
Kirsch, cognac or orange liqueur	15 ml	1 tbsp	1 tbsp

Soak the apricots for several hours in a pot of water. Bring the water to the boil and cook until the apricots are soft. Drain and purée in a food processor, food mill or pass through a sieve. Add the sugar and place back on the heat and cook until the sugar is dissolved. The sauce should have thickened. Apricots come in varying quality and this will effect how thick the sauce becomes. Thin the sauce with orange and lemon juice, using more if necessary. If the sauce is thin, then use only the amount of orange and lemon juice needed to make the sauce a syrupy consistency. When the sauce cools, add the kirsch or cognac. It will keep for a week in the refrigerator.

To serve Serve either warmed or cold.

SAUCE AUX ANANAS
Pineapple Sauce

For ice creams or sorbets, pineapple mousse or fruit-filled crêpes

Ripe fresh pineapple mixed with sugar and rum give a hint of the South Seas to this sauce. It will keep for several days in the refrigerator.

Preparation time: 10 minutes   To serve 6

INGREDIENTS	METRIC	IMPERIAL	AMERICAN
Fresh ripe pineapple	½	½	½
Castor sugar	100 g	4 oz	½ cup
Light rum	50 ml	2 fl oz	¼ cup
Juice from lemon	1	1	1

Cut the pineapple into quarters, core and cut into chunks. Purée in a food processor or liquidiser. Blend in the sugar, rum and lemon juice.

Hint *If using a liquidiser, then add all the ingredients at once and blend.*

Mix all the ingredients thoroughly. Leave to sit for about an hour so that the flavours can blend. The sauce will keep for 2–3 days in the refrigerator.

To serve Serve in a sauce boat or spooned over the dessert.

INDEX OF FRENCH NAMES

INDEX